Stress Management
For the Emergency Care Provider

Alan A. Mikolaj

Montgomery College, The Woodlands, Texas
and
Goldstar EMS, Houston, Texas

Upper Saddle River, New Jersey 07458

Library of Congress Cataloging-in-Publication Data

Mikolaj, Alan A.
   Stress management : for the emergency care provider / Alan A. Mikolaj.
     p. cm.
   Includes bibliographical references and index.
   ISBN 0-13-009686-5
   1. Emergency medical personnel—Job stress. 2. Stress management. I. Title.

RC451.4.E44M54 2004
362.18′01′9—dc22
                                                                              2004008658

Publisher: *Julie Levin Alexander*
Publisher's Assistant: *Regina Bruno*
Senior Acquisitions Editor: *Tiffany Price Salter*
Editorial Assistant: *Joanna Rodzen-Hickey*
Senior Marketing Manager: *Katrin Beacom*
Channel Marketing Manager: *Rachele Strober*
Marketing Coordinator: *Michael Sirinides*
Director of Production and Manufacturing: *Bruce Johnson*
Managing Editor for Production: *Patrick Walsh*
Production Liaison: *Julie Li*
Production Editor: *Karen Ettinger, The GTS Companies/York, PA Campus*
Manufacturing Manager: *Ilene Sanford*
Manufacturing Buyer: *Pat Brown*
Creative Director: *Cheryl Asherman*
Senior Design Coordinator: *Christopher Weigand*
Cover Designer: *Christopher Weigand*
Cover Image: *Getty Images*
Composition: *The GTS Companies/York, PA Campus*
Printing and Binding: *RR Donnelley & Sons*
Cover Printer: *Phoenix Color Corporation*

Credits and acknowledgments borrowed from other sources and reproduced, with permission, in this textbook appear on appropriate page within text.

Copyright © 2005 by Pearson Education, Inc., Upper Saddle River, New Jersey, 07458.
Pearson Prentice Hall. All rights reserved. Printed in the United States of America. This publication is protected by Copyright and permission should be obtained from the publisher prior to any prohibited reproduction, storage in a retrieval system, or transmission in any form or by any means, electronic, mechanical, photocopying, recording, or likewise. For information regarding permission(s), write to: Rights and Permissions Department.

Pearson Prentice Hall™ is a trademark of Pearson Education, Inc.
Pearson® is a registered trademark of Pearson plc
Prentice Hall® is a registered trademark of Pearson Education, Inc.

Pearson Education LTD.   Pearson Education Australia PTY, Limited
Pearson Education Singapore, Pte. Ltd   Pearson Education North Asia Ltd
Pearson Education, Canada, Ltd   Pearson Educación de Mexico, S.A. de C.V.
Pearson Education–Japan   Pearson Education Malaysia, Pte. Ltd

                                                    10 9 8 7 6 5 4 3 2 1
                              ISBN 0-13-009686-5

Dedication

*For all the emergency services workers
And CISM team members
Who dedicate their lives
To serving others.*

Special Thanks to:

Darci Hill, PhD, Sam Houston State University: your inspiration was the seed that made this book possible!

Glenn M. Sanford, PhD, Sam Houston State University: thanks for helping me see the world in a whole new light and providing further impetus in the pursuit of my dreams!

The team members of the Bluebonnet CISM team: your love, acceptance, support, and guidance are invaluable!

The team members of the Southwest Texas CISM team: your love and support taught me so much!

Contents

PREFACE   IX

CHAPTER 1   THE NATURE OF STRESS   1
   STRESS AS A PROCESS   2
   THE FOUR STAGES OF STRESS   4
      STRESSOR   4
      THREAT PERCEPTION   4
      THE STRESS RESPONSE   4
      RELAXATION OR EXHAUSTION   8
   STRESS: GOOD OR BAD?   9
   COPING WITH STRESS   9

CHAPTER 2   EFFECTIVE STRESS MANAGEMENT TECHNIQUES   12
   IMMEDIATE STRESS INTERVENTION STRATEGIES   13
      A HEALTHY DIET   13
      THINGS TO AVOID   15
      EXERCISE   16
      COMMUNICATION   17
      RELAXATION TECHNIQUES   17
   LONG-TERM INTERVENTIONS   20
      COGNITIVE RESTRUCTURING   21

    BEHAVIOR MODIFICATION   21
    ART THERAPY   21

CHAPTER 3 EMERGENCY SERVICES STRESS   23
  UNREALISTIC OPTIMISM   24
  ENVIRONMENTAL STRESSORS   25
  PERSONALITY STRESSORS   26
  OTHER STRESSORS   28
  BURNOUT   29

CHAPTER 4 CRITICAL INCIDENTS   32
  EXPOSURE TO CRITICAL INCIDENTS   33
  COMMON FEATURES OF CRITICAL INCIDENTS   35
    KNOWING OR IDENTIFYING WITH VICTIMS   36
    LARGE-SCALE INCIDENTS   36
    SURPRISE OR NOVELTY   37
  REACTIONS TO CRITICAL INCIDENTS   37

CHAPTER 5 POSTTRAUMATIC STRESS DISORDER   41
  HISTORICAL EVOLUTION OF THE DIAGNOSTIC CRITERIA OF PTSD   42
    DSM-I   44
    DSM-II   44
    DSM-III   45
    DSM-III-R   45
  CURRENT UNDERSTANDING OF PTSD   46
    DSM-IV   46
    PERSONALITY AND TRAUMA   47
  CLOSING   48

CHAPTER 6 CRITICAL INCIDENT STRESS MANAGEMENT   50
  CORE ELEMENTS OF CISM   51
    PRECRISIS PREPARATION   52
    DEMOBILIZATION PROCEDURES   52
    INDIVIDUAL ACUTE CRISIS COUNSELING   52
    DEFUSINGS   53
    CRITICAL INCIDENT STRESS DEBRIEFING   53
    PROCESS DEBRIEFING   54
    FAMILY CRISIS INTERVENTION   56
    FOLLOW-UPS AND REFERRALS   57

CHAPTER 7 CISD: A CRITICAL ANALYSIS 60
  RESEARCH AND THE SCIENTIFIC METHOD 61
    KEY ELEMENTS OF REPORTED RESEARCH 62
  RESEARCH AND CISD 64
    META-ANALYSIS REPORTS 65
    THE SAMPLE AND RANDOMIZATION QUANDARY 67
    LIMITATIONS OF OUTCOME MEASURES 68
    STUDIES OF SPECIAL MENTION 69
    CONCLUSIONS ON THE EFFICACY AND USE OF CISD AND PD 71

GLOSSARY 73

POSTTEST 76

ANSWERS TO POSTTEST 80

APPENDIX A DSM-IV DIAGNOSTIC CRITERIA
FOR ACUTE STRESS DISORDER (ASD) 81

APPENDIX B THE FORMAL CISD PROCESS
CONSISTS OF SEVEN STAGES OR PHASES 85

APPENDIX C CISM: THE SEVEN CORE ELEMENTS 87

APPENDIX D INTERNATIONAL CRITICAL INCIDENT
STRESS FOUNDATION, INC. 89

APPENDIX E REFERENCES 90

BIBLIOGRAPHY 92

INDEX 99

Preface

Stress has been correlated with everything from illness and disease to personality changes, substance abuse, divorce, and even death. Over twenty years ago, when I embarked on my career in the emergency services as an emergency dispatcher, we did not have a complete grasp of the impact that stress and critical incidents have on emergency services providers. Since then, I have worked in the military prehospital environment, on an orthopedic surgical ward, and in many emergency rooms. I have practiced as a paramedic in civilian 911 EMS systems, taught prehospital–emergency medicine at the community college and university levels, and worked offshore and for private EMS services.

During that time, I have taught and worked closely with EMS personnel, firefighters, law enforcement personnel, special operations forces medics, hospital staff, and a host of other specialty emergency rescuers. In the mid-1990s, I was part of a wonderful group of people who founded the **critical incident stress management (CISM)** team serving the greater San Antonio, Texas, area. Since that time, I have participated in numerous debriefings and defusings, and currently volunteer with Bluebonnet CISM in Houston, Texas.

Reflecting on these experiences causes me to recall the stress and trauma I have seen in many emergency services workers. I have seen how appropriate stress management techniques can help build better lives, and I have seen how inappropriate techniques can damage or destroy lives. During that time, the emergence of CISM and an increased focus on emergency services stress have brought encouraging changes to the emergency services. CISM is a relatively new and revitalizing aspect to one of the most stressful yet rewarding occupations of our times.

Over the last forty years, our understanding of stress, its effects on the human condition, and how to manage it have advanced and improved. In particular, we have begun to focus on emergency services workers and the stress associated with what they do. Emergency services workers include firefighters, law enforcement, EMS personnel, dispatchers, and other emergency and rescue specialists. Undeniably, they are exposed to a multitude of stressors that most people cannot even imagine. None of these stressors are more potentially traumatic and life changing than critical incidents. This book examines the phenomena of stress and critical incident stress in the emergency services professions. It explores the latest in stress management techniques as well as the discussions and controversies in the literature.

When our stress response is chronically activated, or "gets stuck," the same responses designed to protect us can become harmful—even lethal. In addition to posttraumatic stress disorder (PTSD), the mark of stress can result in substance abuse, depression, divorce, loss of employment, short- and long-term illnesses, and even suicide. One of the first steps in the prevention of these negative sequelae is education and understanding. More than ever, it is necessary to educate administrators, mental health professionals, medical professionals, emergency services workers themselves, and their families about stress, emergency services stress, critical incident stress, and the intervention programs that are available to them. Critical incident stress management (CISM) teams and organizational human resource personnel provide emergency services workers with an array of services, typically free of charge.

This book begins with an overview of stress, the stress response, and effective stress management techniques. Immediate coping strategies such as healthy diet, exercise, communication, relaxation techniques, and meditative prayer, as well as long-term interventions, are presented. It then highlights the nature of emergency services stress, and how those elements can make emergency services workers more vulnerable to the effects of critical incidents. Critical incidents are defined, and the most recent information available about their impact on emergency services workers is reviewed. The historical evolution of the diagnostic criteria of posttraumatic stress disorder (PTSD) and the current understanding of this pathology is reviewed. The seven elements of CISM—precrisis preparation and education, demobilization procedures, individual acute crisis counseling, defusings, critical incident stress debriefing (CISD), family crisis intervention, and follow-up procedures and referrals—are presented. Finally, a special chapter presents an overview of the scientific method and then presents a critical analysis of the literature regarding CISD and emergency services providers.

I would like to thank the reviewers who provided invaluable comments and suggestions. They are Rhonda Beck, NREMT-P, Central Georgia Technical College; Tony Crystal, Lake Land College; S. Christopher Suprun, Jr., NREMT-P, George Washington University; Harvey Conner, AS, NREMT-P; Robert Hancock, L.P., MSIV, B.S.; K.C. Jones, BSE, NREMT-P, North Arkansas College; Attila Hertelendy, BHSc, CCEMT-P, NREMT-P, University of Mississippi Medical Center; John Picker, MA, LPC, LCDC, Creative Therapy Center; Susie Reierson, MA, LPC, United States Postal Service Employee Assistance Program; and Lisa Hedrick, RN, Bayshore Medical Center.

1

The Nature of Stress

OBJECTIVES

- Name the original pioneer of stress research.
- Identify the general adaptation syndrome.
- Define stress, acute stress, and chronic stress.
- List and describe the four stages of stress.
- Identify the purpose of the stress response.
- Describe the physiological, cognitive, emotional, and behavioral responses to stress.
- Define coping.
- Describe aggression, learned helplessness, avoidance, giving up, and approach coping.

Recent research indicates that approximately 80% of all diseases and illnesses are stress related (Seaward, 1994). Those that are most notably stress related are coronary heart disease, cancer, hypertension, arthritis, and the common cold, to name only a few. Although stress is not the direct cause of these diseases, the influence of stress weakens the body's physiological systems, thus rapidly advancing the disease process.

STRESS AS A PROCESS

When we think about stress, we may recall a period in our life that was stressful, a particular incident that was stressful, or a current problem that is causing some difficulty. What is stress? In their research in the early 1980s, Baum, Grunberg, and Singer (1982) endorsed the idea of stress as a process that is multidimensional. Further integrating the research on stress, others describe it from a living systems approach (Steinberg & Ritzman, 1990). The most accepted definitions of stress today consider it an interactive and multidimensional process with four stages.

Hans Selye, a Canadian physiologist and endocrinologist, was the original pioneer in stress research. He originally named the physiologic response to stress the **general adaptation syndrome (GAS)** (Selye, 1956). He defined stress as the nonspecific response of the body to any demand placed upon it to adapt, whether that demand is pleasurable or painful. Stress may be differentiated between *eustress*, *distress*, and *neustress*. **Eustress** is stress that is perceived as good or pleasant. Winning the lottery would certainly be pleasant, but it would also place some great demands on you to change and adapt to the lucky windfall. **Distress** is stress perceived as bad or unpleasant. Most of us have no difficulty identifying what distress is. **Neustress** is simply neutral stimuli. It is neither pleasant nor unpleasant. Although he named the stages a bit differently than they are referred to today, his seminal research provided great insight into what we call stress.

Richard Lazarus influenced the understanding of stress by asserting that stress is considered a process in which environmental or psychological events, called **stressors**, come to threaten an organism's safety and/or well-being (Lazarus, 1966). Lazarus's work brought a shift of attention from the biological aspects of stress to the perception of the individual. How we perceive an event is crucial. One event may be stressful for one person and not for another. The difference lies in the interpretation of the event and how it affects their lives. After a threatening event is perceived, it is met with a response, part or all of which is directed at reducing the danger or minimizing its effects on the organism.

Brian Seaward, in his comprehensive textbook, *Managing Stress*, points out how stress has been defined differently by various authors over the years. For our purposes, **stress** is defined as the inability to cope with a perceived threat (real or imagined) to one's mental, physical, emotional, and/or spiritual well-being that results in a series of physiological, cognitive, emotional, and behavioral responses and adaptations (coping). When most people talk about stress, they mean *dis*tress. For the purposes of this text, stress will be synonymous with distress, as well.

Stress is further differentiated between *acute stress* (sudden stress) and *chronic stress* (long-term stress). **Acute stress** is more intense and subsides quickly. For example, when someone cuts you off on the highway and nearly hits you, you may experience a sudden increase in heart rate, slight tremors in your hands, a feeling of anger, and a sudden intense focus on the car in front of you and away from music playing on the radio. This is acute stress. Several minutes later when the car is out of sight and the music is back in focus, you are back to being relaxed and enjoying the trip.

Chronic stress, on the other hand, is more sinister and thought to be the real villain. It is the type of stress associated with disease because the body is in a state of arousal for such long periods. It may not be as intense as acute stress, but it can be agonizingly long. Financial troubles are a good example. When credit card bills seem to grow despite regular payments and you do not seem to earn what you need, it will take time, hard work, and probably serious changes to alleviate that chronic stress. It can affect other areas of your life, like your relationships and work, which then causes even more stress. If not dealt with in a healthy and appropriate manner, it can be devastating!

The Four Stages of Stress

Stage 1: Stressor. Something happens that sends a signal, known as a stimulus or a stressor, to the brain, usually via the five senses (the smell of smoke, a scream, a car cutting you off in traffic). Stressors can also be memories, thoughts, or emotions.

Stage 2: Threat Perception. The brain interprets the stimulus as a threat or nonthreat If it is not a threat, the response subsides and ends. However, if it is interpreted as a threat, the nervous and endocrine systems are activated.

Stage 3: The Stress Response. This is the stage where physiological, cognitive, affective, and behavioral responses to the threat perception are manifested. The physiological reaction is also known as the fight-or-flight response originating in the sympathetic nervous system. The nervous and endocrine systems continue to be activated and the body resists the threat until the threat is perceived as a nonthreat, or organs begin to be overwhelmed. Either way, one of two possible outcomes in the fourth stage occurs.

Stage 4: Relaxation or Exhaustion. The body returns to homeostasis, a state of dynamic balance or calm in the body, or it becomes overwhelmed and organs may dysfunction or death occurs.

Adapted from B. L. Seaward, Managing Stress: Principles and Strategies for Health and Wellbeing, *1994: Jones and Bartlett Publishers, Sudbury, MA.* www.jbpub.com. *Adapted with permission.*

THE FOUR STAGES OF STRESS

Stressor

The stress response starts with an environmental or psychological event called a **stressor**. A stressor is any stimulus that elicits the stress response. It is a situation, circumstance, or stimulus that occurs, and it is perceived to be a threat. Just about anything can be a stressor. Usually it is something that reaches the brain via the five senses. When we see a car cut us off in traffic, smell smoke inside of our home, hear a loud noise, taste sour milk, or touch something very hot, signals are sent to the brain. Even memories, thoughts, or emotions generated by our own brain can elicit the stress response.

Stimuli reach the nerve receptors of the senses (Smock, 1999). Light stimulates the rods and cones in your eyes. Odorants stimulate chemoreceptors in the nose. Foods stimulate chemoreceptors on the tongue and in back of the throat. Sound waves vibrate the eardrum that ultimately converts the wave to electrochemical energy. Various sensations stimulate the pain and mechanoreceptors of touch. These signals are then sent either directly to various parts of the brain, or to the spinal cord and then to the brain.

Threat Perception

Remember the last time you had an important job interview or had to talk in front of a large group of people? The simple psychological *idea* of an interview or of public speaking can cause a great deal of stress, just as can noise, smoke, injury, or other physical stressors. Stressors directly threaten *or* cause a perception of threat to our safety or well-being. In other words, there does not have to be a physical threat or trauma to induce the fight-or-flight stress response. Simply thinking about something can be enough stimuli to cause stress.

With lightning speed, the brain interprets these stimuli. The time it takes for someone to pull out in front of you and for your body to react seems almost instantaneous. However, measurable neural responses have taken place. The brain takes in the information, processes it in various locations, and if a threat is perceived, the stress response is activated.

The Stress Response

After the stressor is perceived as being a threat, a reaction occurs called the **stress response**. The purpose of the stress response is to reduce the danger or minimize the effects on the organism. Neurons in the brain send signals to the body activating some systems and minimizing others. The stress response causes changes in physical processes, thoughts, emotions, and behavior. We feel different when we are stressed. Whether the stressor is physical or psychological in nature, the stress response is essentially the same.

Physiological Reactions. The complex physiological response to stress was named the **fight-or-flight** response in 1914 by physiologist Walter Canon. It is called that because it activates systems that prepare our body for a fight that will defend ourselves against a threat or to run away from a threat. When stimuli reach certain areas of the brain, neural pathways connect to our sympathetic nervous system, which then activates part of the endocrine system, the system responsible for the release of hormones. Within seconds of perceiving a threat, hormones—namely epinephrine (adrenaline), norepinephrine, and cortisol—are excreted into the bloodstream causing changes that prepare the body to deal with the stress.

The heart beats stronger and faster to deliver more blood. Some people can actually feel a "wave" move across their chest and the stronger beat of their heart. Breathing increases to provide more oxygen. Blood is shunted away from digestion to vessels in the large muscles to prepare for action. This can cause the feeling of "butterflies" in the stomach or a dry mouth when we are stressed. Arteries in our arms and legs constrict and the blood clots more quickly, so that less blood will be lost if we become wounded or injured. Fats (cholesterol and triglycerides) and glucose (sugar) are pumped into the blood for energy. The increased blood flow to the extremities and increased energy sources causes some people's hands to shake. Perspiration increases to cool the body. Pupils dilate to allow more light in and hearing acuity increases. Immediate states of stress increase immune activity; however, chronic stress decreases immune activity making us vulnerable to a variety of diseases and conditions. Prolonged effects from hormones and the stress response can last minutes to weeks or even months (Mitchel & Bray, 1994; Ornish, 1990; Seaward, 1994). This immediate hyperalert response allows a person to fight off or to escape from a stressor.

Cognitive Reactions. The physical changes associated with stress can be confusing and even frightening. The barrage of physical changes begins to affect cognitions (the way we think) and affective states (emotions or the way we feel). Short-term memory and concentration decrease in times of stress. Minor problems can suddenly become great barriers to overcome. Our sense of humor diminishes and criticism is taken more harshly. It can be difficult to think clearly and our vulnerability to additional stress increases. The event or stressor is oftentimes played repeatedly in our minds. People frequently blame others for the stress and their own confusing and distressing reactions.

> **Physiological Reactions to Stress**
> **(The Fight-or-Flight Response)**
>
> - Increased heart rate
> - Increased blood pressure
> - increased respirations
> - Vasodilation of arteries in large muscles
> - Tremors or shakes
> - Increased serum glucose
> - Increased cholesterol
> - Increased triglycerides
> - Increased muscular strength
> - Increased perspiration
> - Pupil dilation
> - Initial immune system increase
> - Decreased gastric movement
> - Nausea and vomiting
> - Diarrhea
> - Dry mouth
> - Fatigue
> - Sleep disturbances

Adapted from J. Mitchell and G. Bray, Emergency Services Stress: Guidelines on Preserving the Health and Careers of Emergency Services Personnel, *1st edition. © 1990. Adapted by permission of Pearson Education, Inc., Upper Saddle River, NJ and from B. L. Seaward,* Managing Stress: Principles and Strategies for Health and Wellbeing, *1994: Jones and Bartlett Publishers, Sudbury, MA.* www.jbpub.com. *Adapted with permission.*

Have you ever been late getting ready to go somewhere really important? You are in a hurry to leave and suddenly you cannot find your car keys. The more you look, the more frustrated and late you become. If someone tries to make some suggestions on where to look or tries to make light of the situation to ease the tension, you may snap back and get even more upset. Suddenly, the only thing that matters in your world is finding those darn keys! You might even accuse someone of moving them. If someone tries to suggest a way to prevent losing the keys in the future, you might not take the suggestion very well. These are all cognitive reactions in a stressful situation.

Affective or Emotional Reactions. The changes in cognition are accompanied by a wide variety of affective or emotional responses. Stressors can directly and indirectly trigger changes in the limbic portions of the brain responsible for emotion. A sense of absentmindedness, forgetfulness, and the inability to concentrate along with the physically aroused hyperalert state leads to two basic emotional responses: anger and fear. Anger produces the urge to fight, and fear promotes the urge to run and hide. Angry outbursts, panic reactions, denial, guilt, hopelessness, or a sense of being overwhelmed, lost, abandoned, or alone are all common emotional reactions to stress. Feeling like no one understands what we are going through is quite common. The intensity of these emotions depends largely upon the stressor and the perception of the threat.

Cognitive Reactions to Stress

- Decreased short-term memory
- Decrease in concentration
- Confusion
- Lowered attention span
- Repeated thoughts or images
- Diminished sense of humor
- Calculation difficulties
- Disruption in logical thinking
- Minor problems seem unmanageable
- Criticism taken more harshly
- Absentmindedness
- Forgetfulness

Adapted from J. Mitchell and G. Bray, Emergency Services Stress: Guidelines on Preserving the Health and Careers of Emergency Services Personnel, *1st edition. © 1990. Adapted by permission of Pearson Education, Inc., Upper Saddle River, NJ and from B. L. Seaward,* Managing Stress: Principles and Strategies for Health and Wellbeing, *1994: Jones and Bartlett Publishers, Sudbury, MA. www.jbpub.com. Adapted with permission.*

Emotional Reactions to Stress

- Anger
- Fear
- Frustration
- Feeling overwhelmed
- Loss of control
- Worry
- Denial
- Panic reactions
- Feeling lost, abandoned, or alone
- Guilt
- Depression or sadness
- Hopelessness

Adapted from J. Mitchell and G. Bray, Emergency Services Stress: Guidelines on Preserving the Health and Careers of Emergency Services Personnel, *1st edition. © 1990. Adapted by permission of Pearson Education, Inc., Upper Saddle River, NJ and from B. L. Seaward,* Managing Stress: Principles and Strategies for Health and Wellbeing, *1994: Jones and Bartlett Publishers, Sudbury, MA. www.jbpub.com. Adapted with permission.*

Behavioral Reactions. With all of these physiological, cognitive, and emotional changes, it is no surprise that stress changes our behavior. Withdrawal, angry outbursts, crying, hyperactivity, changes in interactions with others, increased smoking, alcohol, caffeine, or illegal substances, excessive or inappropriate humor, and changes in communication could all be part of the behavioral changes in the stress response.

Just watch people who are late for work in rush-hour traffic. Their driving behavior is much different from when the very same people are driving to church on Sunday morning or out to a relaxed dinner. You can see quick accelerations and stops, frequent lane changes, cutting people off, and yelling. Stress changes behavior.

Relaxation or Exhaustion

At some point, the stressor is eliminated, one escapes, or the stress continues until organs can no longer maintain the stress response. If the stressor is removed in time (or the perception of threat changes), the body can return to its usual state of dynamic equilibrium or **homeostasis**. The heart rate slows down, blood pressure returns to normal, and cholesterol levels drop. The body can now go about the business of the day.

Behavioral Reactions to Stress

- Angry outbursts
- Crying
- Violence
- Change in communication
- Increased smoking, alcohol, or caffeine
- Illegal substance use and/or abuse
- Inappropriate humor
- Unusual silence
- Withdrawal
- Oversuspiciousness
- Unusual behavior
- Increased alertness to surroundings

Adapted from J. Mitchell and G. Bray, Emergency Services Stress: Guidelines on Preserving the Health and Careers of Emergency Services Personnel, *1st edition. © 1990. Adapted by permission of Pearson Education, Inc., Upper Saddle River, NJ and from B. L. Seaward,* Managing Stress: Principles and Strategies for Health and Wellbeing, *1994: Jones and Bartlett Publishers, Sudbury, MA. www.jbpub.com. Adapted with permission.*

However, when stress remains constant, a stage of exhaustion occurs. Maintaining homeostasis becomes increasingly difficult. Immune response decreases, and diseases or disease processes begin to weaken organs and organ systems. If the breakdown is chronic, severe, or involves a critical organ or system, the body may even die.

STRESS: GOOD OR BAD?

Interestingly, the stress response can be lifesaving in a dangerous emergency. It gives us the energy to protect and defend ourselves, or to withdraw if the threat is too severe. It is sometimes a healthy and normal reaction and works best for situations in which the danger is clear, well defined, and short term,

A. T. W. Simeons (1961), a disciple of Hans Selye, suggests that the stress response is outdated. Seen as a defense mechanism that has not kept up with the evolutionary development of the human mind, it just does not serve us well in many of our modern stressful situations. When our stress response becomes chronically activated, or "gets stuck," the same responses designed to protect us can become harmful—even lethal. Dean Ornish, MD (1990), renowned cardiologist, researcher, and author, stated it well (italics in the original):

> But *what begins as protective can itself become destructive if the walls always remain up.* By analogy, the fight-or-flight response, which starts out as being protective and necessary to our survival, can become harmful or even lethal to us if the fight-or-flight response is chronically turned on, as though saber-toothed tigers are lurking around every corner. (p. 179)

In addition to the physiological, cognitive, affective, and behavioral reactions to stress, some researchers have investigated the role of genetics, personality traits, and culture in stress. Although there is some variance attributable to these factors, all humans experience stress and stress reactions. So, while the fight-or-flight stress response can be lifesaving, it can have detrimental effects, as well.

COPING WITH STRESS

Coping or **coping styles** refer to efforts used to reduce or manage the demands created by stressors and the stress response. Coping efforts can be healthy or unhealthy, effective or ineffective. Oftentimes when we hear people talking about coping, we interpret it to mean that someone was able to cope effectively with their stress. For example, we might hear someone say, "John is coping with his problems." John might not be coping in a healthy or effective manner. He might be coping by abusing alcohol or lashing out at others.

One tactic people use is **aggression.** Some people advocate the motto, "Just get it out." This is an extreme form of an idea that originated with the famous physiologist and founder of psychoanalytic psychology, Sigmund Freud. Freud espoused the idea that catharsis relieves symptoms. According to Freud, catharsis was the release of pent-up emotions through talking about forgotten memories and feelings. Freud's cathartic process was designed to take place in a safe environment, with a professional, and over a long period of time. Research today demonstrates that acting out aggressive behavior, or "just getting it out," does not lead to the relief of the symptoms of stress. Aggressive behavior simply leads to more anger and creates more interpersonal conflicts and problems. Other coping strategies associated with limited value are self-blame, negative self-talk, and excessive self-indulgences in food, drugs, or alcohol.

Learned helplessness, avoidance, and giving up are similar phenomena that may have limited coping value. Martin Seligman is well known for his work describing **learned helplessness**. When people come to believe that a negative or stressful event is out of their control, they may become apathetic, depressed, and give up. Unfortunately, learned helplessness is oftentimes generalized to other situations. Soon, a person could be responding routinely by passively accepting negative events and becoming depressed.

A similar type of coping is **avoidance coping**. This line of attack involves avoiding things, people, or thoughts associated with the stressor. The objective is to distract oneself from the stressor. This can be either effective or ineffective, depending on the situation. When a situation is uncontrollable or immediate, this line of defense can be effective. It can allow you to maintain focus and address whatever may be coming up next. For example, ignoring pain when dealing with a violent patient or subject can allow one to handle the immediate situation. While helpful in the immediate crisis, it is important to remember that avoidance coping styles are not generally associated with long-term, effective stress reduction.

Some people have negative feelings about another type of avoidance coping: **giving up**. It carries some negative connotations in many circles. However, the idea of giving up is not necessarily an ineffective coping strategy. There are times when giving up may be effective. For example, you could find yourself in a situation in which you are working and going to school full time. The demands of both endeavors begin to affect your grades and performance at work. It might be better to drop a course or two and reduce the demands than to continue a downward spiral that might result in unfavorable consequences.

Approach coping styles are generally associated with better adaptation to stress. This type of strategy involves meeting the stressor head-on. People who use approach coping intensify their efforts to understand, process, and deal with a stressful situation. There are many ways to utilize approach coping strategies: obtaining information to increase understanding, confronting a situation, rehearsing a plan in your mind, communicating, seeing the situation differently, learning something from the situation, to name but a few. In the next chapter, we explore some specific and effective stress management techniques used today.

Key Points

- Stress is the inability to cope with a perceived threat (real or imagined) to one's mental, physical, emotional, and/or spiritual well-being that results in a series of physiological, cognitive, emotional, and behavioral responses and adaptations.
- Stress is further differentiated between *acute stress*, which is sudden, more intense, and subsides quickly, and *chronic stress*, which is long-term stress and associated with disease.
- Stress is divided into four stages: the stressor, a threat perception, the stress response, and relaxation or exhaustion.
- The stress response is directed at reducing the danger or minimizing the effects on an organism, and causes changes in physical processes, cognitive processes, affective states, and behavior.
- The stress response causes physiological, cognitive, affective, and behavioral reactions.
- Chronic stress can be harmful and potentially even fatal to an organism.
- Strategies for dealing with stress that may have limited value are aggression, learned helplessness, self-blame, negative self-talk, and excessive self-indulgence in food, drugs, or alcohol.
- Other coping strategies are avoidance coping and approach coping.
- Approach coping styles are generally associated with better adaptation to stress.

2
Effective Stress Management Techniques

OBJECTIVES

- Differentiate between immediate and long-term stress interventions.
- Define the holistic approach to managing stress.
- Describe how diet and exercise affect stress.
- Explain why sugars, caffeine, and alcohol are not recommended, especially during stressful periods.
- Explain how communication, positive relationships, and intimacy are linked to decreased stress.
- Describe the technique of diaphragmatic breathing.
- Describe how to use music therapy to reduce stress.
- List the effects of massage therapy.
- Describe the benefits of using meditative prayer to reduce stress.
- Recognize some of the long-term stress intervention techniques.

Each of us makes use of different ways to help reduce the feeling of stress in our lives. Effective or healthy stress management techniques include two strategies: immediate interventions and long-term interventions. There are some things we can do immediately that will reduce the stress response. The overall goal of these **immediate interventions** is to use what we have on hand to reduce the stress response and return ourselves to a more normal precrisis or prestressed state (Greenstone, 1993). **Long-term interventions** focus more on learning and developing new skills that can be used to reduce the stress response or teach new ways of thinking about the stressors in our lives.

IMMEDIATE STRESS INTERVENTION STRATEGIES

How do you relieve stress? Some people drink alcohol, take illegal drugs, or isolate themselves in front of the TV or computer for hours. Others yell, scream, and break things. Of course, none of these methods would be considered healthy or effective stress management techniques. Most of them would ultimately produce even more stress. Most of the immediate and healthy ways to deal with stress are simple. Rather than relying on any one single technique, a multifaceted or "shotgun" approach seems to work best. The stress response was once thought to be a purely physical response. Then, it was referred to as a mind–body phenomenon. Now, it is understood to be a complex, multifaceted phenomenon involving the mental, physical, emotional, and spiritual components of well-being. This **holistic approach** to managing stress means that we try to heal the *whole* person: body, mind, heart, and spirit. Combining healthy diet, exercise, communication, relaxation techniques, and meditative prayer can do more to help reduce stress than using any one of the techniques alone.

A Healthy Diet

Diet and exercise top the list of what we can do to combat stress. You know an unhealthy diet can lead to all types of health problems. Our diet also affects our ability to fight against stress. In fact, some foods can actually induce or mimic a state of stress. There are three basic types of food the body needs for optimal functioning: fats, carbohydrates, and proteins. In addition, there is one very special nutrient worth mentioning that most of us forget about: water (Kowalski, 1989).

Fats. Fats are a concentrated supply of energy. Fats contain more than twice as much energy as carbohydrates per gram than other foods. They are designed for prolonged, moderately intense activity, like aerobic exercise. As mentioned in chapter 1, when our body is in a stressful state, fats pour through the bloodstream in order to provide energy. Stressful periods by themselves can raise fat levels in the blood to unacceptable levels. Eating fatty foods during stressful periods can seriously raise fat levels in the blood. As Dr. Dean Ornish (1990) points out in his best seller, even a single fatty meal can release a hormone, thromboxane, which causes the arteries to constrict and the blood to clot faster. High levels of fat in the blood are highly correlated with cardiac and other serious vessel diseases, like stroke and peripheral arterial occlusions. Add to this phenomenon increased clotting factors, and we have the building blocks for a heart attack, stroke, or peripheral vascular disease. While it may not always be possible to avoid the fatty, fast foods while on duty, with a little concerted effort, reducing fat intake is achievable. Being particularly aware of it during stressful periods is even more important.

Complex Carbohydrates. So, what should we eat? **Complex carbohydrates,** such as pasta, potatoes, and rice, and fresh fruits and vegetables, are a much healthier choice. They provide more nutrition and are a better fuel source. Mother was right! Eating your fruits and vegetables is good for you. Chronic stress can deplete vitamins and minerals. Fresh fruits and vegetables and enriched complex carbohydrates can be a rich source of vitamins, minerals, and antioxidants that are necessary to metabolize fat and synthesize the stress hormones. In a recent article published in the *Journal of the American Pharmaceutical Association,* June McDermott (2000) points out that

> There appear to be significant health benefits from dietary antioxidants, as can be found in fruits and vegetables . . . Overall, it appears that antioxidant nutrients, especially those from food sources, have important roles in preventing pathogenic processes related to cancer, cardiovascular disease, macular degeneration, cataracts, and asthma, and may enhance immune function. (p. 785)

Water. If asked to name the nutrient essential for health and life, few people would mention **water**. Yet this essential nutrient accounts for most of the body's weight and is used in every cell and chemical process in the body. It has so many functions in the body that discussing them all is not appropriate here. It is important to mention a few things about water and stress. Remember the old advice to drink eight 8-ounce glasses of water each day? Well, that wisdom is just as true today, and if you're stressed, even more so. Water is essential to flush out the harmful chemicals produced by stress and return the body to **homeostasis** (normal, balanced state). Your body can absorb water from other fluids such as juices and milk. Remember, however, if a beverage is caffeinated or alcoholic, it will deplete the body of much needed water.

Things to Avoid

There are drinks, foods, and food products we should try to avoid, especially during stressful periods: sugar, caffeine, and alcohol.

Processed or Simple Sugars. Simple sugars are found in candy, jams, table sugar, honey, and sodas. They are referred to as empty calories because they have been stripped of their nutritional value during the refining process. In addition, they tend to deplete essential vitamin stores. They create fluctuations in blood glucose levels, causing fatigue, headaches, and irritability. Fluctuating blood glucose and irritability can mimic, induce, or add to the stress response.

Caffeine. Caffeine is the most widely used stimulant in the world (Comer, 1998). Caffeine contains a substance, **methylated xanthine**, which acts like a fight-or-flight stimulator. Not only does it make us hyperalert, it can make us more susceptible to stress and reduce much needed water in the body. Caffeine is found in many foods, including coffee, tea, chocolate, and many sodas. Research indicates that a 12-ounce cup of coffee has enough caffeine to evoke an adverse arousal of the central nervous system.

Alcohol. Ronald Comer (1998) points out something we have known about alcohol for a very long time. **Alcohol** is a central nervous system depressant and is highly addictive. This potentially dangerous and toxic chemical gets into our brain and begins depressing the higher centers of the brain that control judgment and inhibition. As more alcohol is ingested, it depresses other areas in the brain, causing confusion, less restrained behaviors, and a sense of euphoria (Smock, 1999). It causes increased urination and dehydration. The ability to make rational judgments declines, speech becomes less guarded and less coherent, and memory falters. Motor impairment becomes more pronounced and reaction times slow. Eventually, coma and death can occur at blood levels of 0.55% (Comer, 1998). These are hardly the effects one needs when under stress.

The long-term effects of alcohol on the body include liver damage, immune system depression, depletions of vitamins B that cause brain damage (Wernicke's encephalopathy and Korsakoff's syndrome), and eventually death. The depressant effects of alcohol do *not* cause any positive changes to the stress response or make the stressors vanish. In fact, alcohol is a factor in more than a third of all suicides, homicides, assaults, rapes, and accidental deaths, including close to half of all fatal automobile accidents (Seaward, 1994). The impact on personal and family relationships can be devastating and lifelong. Alcohol will temporarily numb the brain. When it wears off, the stress remains, and more than likely, new stressors appear. Although a complete discussion of alcoholism is not appropriate here, if emergency services workers find that they have to drink alcohol to manage stress, use alcohol, or any other substance to cope, they are probably in emotional pain and need professional support. Therefore, reducing fats, simple sugars, caffeine, and alcohol are effective immediate *and* long-term stress intervention techniques.

Exercise

Since the stress response prepares the body for physical exertion, one of the best ways to return the body to homeostasis is to exercise. For immediate stress management, it is *not* recommended that you start a new, intense, exercise program unless you first consult with your physician. Activities that brought you enjoyment before the stressful period like going for walks in your neighborhood, playing tennis, or going for a bicycle ride, are best. Of course, if you are in the habit of regular, vigorous exercise, continue! For overall stress management, initiating a professionally guided, complete, exercise program is recommended and can help reduce stress in so many ways.

Some of the benefits of regular, vigorous exercise are decreased resting heart rate, blood pressure, muscle tension, cholesterol, body fat and weight, and aging. Those who regularly exercise have lower anxiety, less depression, and increased resistance to the physiological and emotional consequences of stress (Salmon, 2001). While those who exercise regularly still have a stress response to stressors, the response is usually less intense and they recover from the harmful effects of stress much quicker.

Immediate Stress Intervention Strategies

- Avoiding fat in your diet
- Eating complex carbohydrates
- Drinking plenty of water
- Avoiding simple sugars
- Avoiding or reducing caffeine intake
- Avoiding or eliminating alcohol
- Regular, vigorous physical exercise
- Communicate about stressful events in your life in a variety of forums
- Utilize diaphragmatic breathing techniques
- Engage in music therapy
- Meditative prayer

Communication

Communication, positive relationships, and intimacy are linked to decreased stress, happiness, healing, and longevity. In his best-selling book on reversing heart disease, Dean Ornish, MD, discussed many studies that all concluded socially isolated people have a two- to three-fold increased risk of death from *all* causes when compared to those who felt most connected to others. Just being a member of a club, church, or synagogue decreased the risk of premature death (Ornish, 1990).

A series of studies (Pennebaker & Susman, 1988; Pennebaker, Hughes, & O'Heeron, 1987) were conducted at Southern Methodist University in Dallas. It was concluded that the inhibition of thoughts, feelings, or behaviors increases autonomic nervous system activity (the stress response) in the short term, and that over time, it increases the probability of disease. It was further concluded that sharing feelings increased immune system activity. In other words, hiding your feelings and thoughts in order to be "tough," or whatever reason, is not a healthy stress management technique. Whether writing in a private journal, talking things over with a friend, loved one, or trained professional, communication about the stressor and the stress helps reduce the stress response and boost the immune system. Failing to confide in someone about traumatic events leads to stress and long-term health problems.

Part of the problem with communication is that few of us have been trained to use empathic, healing communication techniques. Communication can be both an immediate and a long-term stress intervention strategy. Learning communication skills from a trained professional are a long-term intervention strategy that is highly recommended.

Relaxation Techniques

There are some simple relaxation techniques that reduce the stress response and can be used right away: diaphragmatic breathing, music therapy, massage therapy, and exercise.

Diaphragmatic Breathing. Deep breathing or **diaphragmatic breathing** is the easiest method of relaxation to practice. You can do it just about anywhere, anytime. Follow the simple steps below to use this stress-reducing technique.

Music Listening Practice. **Music listening practice** is the use of music to bring about helpful changes in our emotional or physical health (Seaward, 1994). There are several theories that explain why music

Diaphragmatic Breathing

- Loosening tight clothing will help, and a quiet environment is best.
- While sitting up straight or lying down on your back, close your eyes.
- Turn your attention to your breathing.
- Begin inhaling, preferably through your nose, but you can use your mouth.
- Focus the inhalation to the deepest part of your lungs and abdomen, causing your abdomen to rise first. As you are beginning, you can place a hand on your upper abdomen and try to push it up or out with your inhalation. Then move to filling your midchest and finally the top part of the chest.
- Hold or pause the breath slightly. As you progress, you may want to hold for a four-count.
- Slowly begin releasing the air from your lungs in a slow, relaxed fashion.
- Pause slightly, before the next inhalation.
- Repeat this several times for an immediate stress relief.

Adapted from D. Ornish, Dr. Dean Ornish's Program for Reversing Heart Disease, *1990: Random House. Adapted with permission and B. L. Seaward,* Managing Stress: Principles and Strategies for Health and Wellbeing, *1994: Jones and Bartlett Publishers, Sudbury, MA.* www.jbpub.com. *Adapted with permission.*

listening practice works. While the focus of this discussion does not include these theories, music possesses a strong therapeutic quality. There are a few principles to keep in mind.

The musical selection one chooses for relaxation should meet two criteria to be effective music therapy:

- it must be an instrumental or acoustic selection with a slow tempo, and
- it should be enjoyable rather than disturbing.

No one piece of music will relax everyone equally, so experiment with different pieces, groups, or composers. There are commercially available tapes and compact discs created especially for relaxation that can be purchased at local music outlets, specialty stores, or online. The environment should be quiet and allow full attention to the music. For the most relaxing effect, choose a posture, sitting or reclining, that will facilitate relaxation and focus on the music. Combining diaphragmatic breathing exercises with music listening practice is a great idea. Some people will listen for just a few minutes and others for as long as several hours. Somewhere in between is appropriate for most people.

> ### Music Listening Practice
>
> - Choose instrumental or acoustic music with a slow tempo.
> - The selection should be enjoyable.
> - Find a quiet environment conducive to relaxation.
> - Use a sitting or reclining posture.
> - Combine diaphragmatic breathing while listening to the selection.

Adapted from B. L. Seaward, Managing Stress: Principles and Strategies for Health and Wellbeing, *1994: Jones and Bartlett Publishers, Sudbury, MA.* www.jbpub.com. *Adapted with permission.*

Massage Therapy. Another highly effective relaxation technique, **massage therapy**, has been in use for over 3,000 years. The need for human touch has been well established. Massage therapy has been associated with a reduction in heart rate, decreased stress response, and decreased anxiety. It is also correlated with enhanced immune system function. Perhaps the most notable and profound effect of massage therapy is the state of complete physical relaxation one experiences during and immediately following the experience. Professional therapeutic massage therapists are either certified or licensed through a state agency, and can have affiliation or membership with the American Massage Therapy Association ("About AMTA," 2000). Choose your massage therapist as you would any other professional.

Meditative Prayer. Every culture and every major religion in the world has some form of **meditative prayer** or self-reflective practice, including Buddhism, Catholicism, Confucianism, Hinduism, Islam, Judaism, Native Americans, Protestantism, and Taoism. Initially, meditative prayer has a calming effect on the mind's basic thought processes. Once this is achieved, a deeper series of layers is unveiled to reveal insights into the self or soul with a sense of connecting to the Divine. With regular practice, these insights become more revealing and the connection to the Divine so complete that a spiritual transformation may occur, resulting in a state that has been called enlightenment, nirvana, rapture, transcendence, a path with heart (Kornfield, 1993), or simply, awareness (De Mello, 1992).

Physiological and psychological effects of meditative prayer have been studied since the 1970s (Seaward, 1994). Among some of the effects known to occur are decreased heart rate, breathing, blood pressure, muscle tension, and oxygen consumption. Increases in skin resistance and brain alpha waves, both indicators of deep relaxation, also occur. Participants in studies report decreases in smoking, alcohol consumption, and recreational drug use, and sleep more soundly.

Above all else, participants regularly report a greater sense of general well-being or inner peace.

If you want more information about meditative prayer, a plethora of material is available through bookstores, churches, the Internet, and even in the yellow pages. There are various types of meditation such as exclusive, inclusive, transcendental, and Zen meditation, among others. You may want to investigate a few methods before you choose one that fits your personal spirituality and/or religious needs best.

LONG-TERM INTERVENTIONS

Long-term interventions focus on learning and developing new skills that can be used to reduce the stress response. These techniques have the most lasting and deep-rooted effects. They are techniques that are more formal and usually require the help of a professional or enrolling in a training program or therapy. Long-term stress intervention techniques will require more work on your part, but the benefits are tremendous!

Long-term interventions can positively impact careers, relationships, and provide strategies for dealing with much more than stress. While it is beyond the scope of this text to address these interventions in detail, we will touch on just a few of them. Please seek a licensed therapist, psychologist, psychiatrist, or other appropriate professional to inquire about these interventions. See the following box for a partial listing of long-term interventions.

Long-Term Stress Intervention Techniques

- Cognitive restructuring
- Behavior modification
- Journal writing
- Art therapy
- Communication skills training
- Time management
- Dream therapy
- Hatha yoga
- Mental imagery
- T'ai Chi Ch'uan
- Biofeedback
- Progressive muscular relaxation

Cognitive Restructuring

Cognitive restructuring was pioneered by such reputable researchers and authors as Albert Ellis, Bernie Sigel, MD, Walter Scafer, Victor Frankl, and Roger Allen. This model assists people with implementing lifestyle and behavioral changes through changes in thought processes. The model resonates some of the knowledge from self-awareness techniques and utilizes inner dialogue, learning new thought processes, and self-affirmation. It entails changing distorted and unrealistic perceptions and patterns into views that are more accurate and have clearer meaning. It is best initiated with the help of a licensed mental health professional who has expertise in this area.

Behavior Modification

You have probably heard of Ivan Pavlov and his famous research on dogs, food, and bells. His research resulted in what today is termed **Pavlovian conditioning** or **classical conditioning** (Baldwin & Baldwin, 1998). Pavlov's influence on psychology and physiology established the groundwork for behaviorism and extends to today's modern understanding of conditioning behaviors and learning. John Watson, considered the founder of behaviorism, wanted psychology to be as scientific as possible (Barlow & Durand, 1999). Another highly influential behaviorist, B. F. Skinner, made contributions that helped establish operant conditioning, reinforcement, and the scientific beginnings of programmed instruction (Thorne & Henley, 1997). There are several types of behavior modification programs or theories currently conducted in the United States that help people with changing negative health habits like smoking or alcoholism, or improving lifestyle with time management or assertiveness skills training. Seeking a qualified mental health professional who has expertise in behaviorism can have positive, life-changing results.

Art Therapy

Art therapy uses the creative process to help people express in a nonverbal manner what they may not be able to verbally express (Seaward, 1994). It also facilitates self-awareness and personal growth. Often, when people are distressed, it is difficult to communicate verbally. Without some type of communication or self-expression, the progress of healing and growth is inhibited. Under the direction of a licensed art therapist, self-expression of both verbal and nonverbal communication can be synthesized and interpreted, allowing a greater sense of personal awareness. Art therapy has been used as an adjunct for many types of situations and conditions to include cancer patients, drug rehabilitation, eating disorders, not to mention managing stress.

In the previous two chapters, we explored the nature of stress and the management techniques available to manage stress. In the next chapter, we examine how the jobs of emergency services providers are particularly stressful.

> ### Key Points
>
> - *Immediate interventions* use what we have on hand to reduce the stress response and return ourselves to a more normal precrisis or prestressed state.
> - *Long-term interventions* focus more on learning and developing new skills that can be used to reduce the stress response or teach new ways of thinking about the stressors in our lives.
> - Combining healthy diet, exercise, communication, relaxation techniques, and meditative prayer are proven effective immediate stress intervention techniques.
> - Avoiding fats, simple sugars, caffeine, and alcohol are effective immediate and long-term stress intervention techniques.
> - Communication is probably the most efficient and effective way to reduce stress.
> - Though more formal and requiring more energy and commitment, long-term intervention strategies have deep-rooted and more lasting effects.

3

Emergency Services Stress

OBJECTIVES

- Define emergency services provider.
- Define unrealistic optimism and how it can adversely affect emergency services providers.
- Identify examples of environmental stressors in emergency services work.
- Identify general personality factors or traits of emergency services providers.
- Describe how being internally motivated, action oriented, possessing a strong need to help others, and a strong sense of dedication can become stressors for the emergency services provider.
- Describe how unpredictability and shift-work are stressors for the emergency services provider.
- Define burnout.
- List the three characteristics of burnout.
- Define depersonalization.
- List the effects of burnout on emergency services providers and those they serve.

Who are emergency services providers? **Emergency services providers** are those who are employed or volunteer in the emergency services profession and their support staff: first responders, firefighters, emergency medical technicians (EMTs), paramedics, law enforcement personnel, dispatchers, hazardous materials specialists, rescue specialists, and others. The scope of these workers has also grown to include those who work in emergency rooms, critical care units, and industrial complexes. Other terms that can be used to describe this occupational group are emergency services workers, emergency workers, emergency services personnel, and emergency personnel.

Emergency services providers are often overdramatized or satirized in the media. The realities and stressors of this work are often not reflected accurately. Some shows that follow the live action of these workers may reveal a more accurate picture; however, it is impossible for the media to grasp the complete experience of what it means to be an emergency services provider.

Emergency services providers may be paid or volunteer paraprofessionals, and are in all parts of urban, suburban, and rural America. They work 8-, 12-, or 24-hour shifts. Oftentimes, they feel compelled to work overtime shifts due to a great sense of dedication and the low wages associated with this work.

The responsibility for the life and safety of others is considered a significant stressor. Emergency services personnel (firefighters, law enforcement, emergency medical providers, and their support personnel) experience tremendous occupational stress (Bryant & Harvey, 1995; Linton, 1995; Mitchell & Bray, 1994; Moran & Colless, 1995; Robinson, Sigman, & Wilson, 1997). The environment of the emergency services worker is a particularly stressful place (Mitchell, 1983). In spite of this, people who choose a career in emergency services have unique personalities that match them to their work. However, the very **traits** that make them great at what they do, also make them more vulnerable to stress and critical incident stress.

UNREALISTIC OPTIMISM

In a study of perceptions of work stress in Australian firefighters, Moran and Colless (1995) reported an unusual dichotomy that some emergency service workers have known for a long time. Firefighters rated their job as more stressful compared with other occupations. However, they also reported their chances of being adversely affected or harmed by this stress as *less* than average. In other words, the firefighters recognize that their jobs are more stressful than other jobs, but they do not think that they are affected by this increased stress. This dichotomy is known as **unrealistic optimism**. It could just as easily be called the Superman syndrome. The patriarchal history of emergency services has led people both inside and outside the emergency services to refer to it as simple *machoism* or *machismo,* although this phenomenon is not isolated to males. In their book, *EMS Stress: An Emergency Responder's Handbook for Living Well,* Ray Shelton and Jack Kelly (1995) refer to aspects of this phenomenon as the "superhuman myth." It is a false perception that "I can do it all," or that one will always be in control. This is a false sense of immunity.

So many emergency services workers use denial as a defense mechanism to protect themselves from stress and critical incident stress. Speaking from a Freudian perspective, James Janik (1992) points out that denying the impact of stress or critical incident stress (see chapter 4) consumes energy that could be better utilized by the mind and handicaps a person's ability to assess problems and cope effectively. This could then lead to cumulative stress problems and even posttraumatic stress disorder.

When anyone, including emergency services workers, hold the false belief that they are not adversely affected by stressors (or are not affected at all), they may not adequately manage the stress response. This can affect their occupational as well as their personal lives. Not only can this lead to chronic stress (and to an increased risk for health and other problems), but it also sets them up for more serious stress reactions in the future. If they are not effectively managing the day-to-day stressors, what happens when something really big happens?

ENVIRONMENTAL STRESSORS

Emergency services providers do not usually work in well-equipped or well-staffed offices or facilities. The immediate environment of the emergency services provider is wrought with stressors. Sirens, cries for help, moans of pain, angry or threatening voices, blaring radios, and roaring engines are examples of noise stressors in the emergency environment. Weather conditions can add aggravation to an already stressful environment. These are examples of **environmental stressors** in emergency services work. Another example is emergency driving. Normal driving can be stressful enough. Emergency driving, traffic, and crowds can frustrate attempts to access victims. Hazardous materials, waiting for "backup," new high technology, intoxicated and abusive victims, bystanders, or patients—all can add tension to emergency services workers' environment (Mitchell & Bray, 1994; Moran & Colles, 1995).

These are the environmental stressors that are most often identified. However, over the years I have heard about other occupational stressors that may cause even more stress: low pay, conflicts with administration (Beaton & Murphy, 1993), lack of respect from other health care professionals, old, outdated, or poorly maintained equipment and vehicles, coworkers, lack of sleep . . . the list is probably endless. When these things add up, emergency services personnel are exposed to high levels of occupational stress. John C. Linton, PhD (1995), from the West Virginia University School of Medicine put it distinctly:

> In addition to having an increased risk of personal injury, they are exposed to grisly scenes and must perform their duties under adverse circumstances: They must consider all bodily fluids as biohazards, contend with administrations often driven by politics, and assist a public with whom litigation is an ever-present threat. (p. 567)

PERSONALITY STRESSORS

Jeffery Mitchell, PhD, outlined personality "factors" very similar to **personality traits** (enduring and consistent ways of thinking, acting, and feeling) common to emergency services providers and labeled them the **rescue personality** (Mitchell & Bray, 1994). He illuminated how these personality factors can become stressors themselves and add to emergency services stress. Some of these traits are being detail-oriented, setting high standards for themselves, being internally motivated, being action-oriented, being quick decision-makers, and possessing intense dedication. See the following box for additional examples of traits of the rescue personality.

General Personality Traits of Emergency Services Providers

- Detail oriented
- Set high standards for themselves
- Quick decision makers
- Need to be in control
- Obsessive (desire to do a perfect job or tendency to "get stuck" on one thing)
- Compulsive (tend to repeat the same actions for very similar events; traditional)
- Highly motivated by internal factors
- Action oriented
- High need for stimulation
- Have a need for immediate gratification
- Easily bored
- Risk takers
- Highly dedicated
- Strong need to be needed

Adapted from J. Mitchell and G. Bray, Emergency Services Stress: Guidelines on Preserving the Health and Careers of Emergency Services Personnel, *1st edition. © 1990. Adapted by permission of Pearson Education, Inc., Upper Saddle River, NJ.*

Emergency service providers are detail oriented and frequently set extremely high standards for themselves. While this helps them to do a better job, it also sets them up for stress. When unusually high standards cannot be met or they are met with perceived failures, frustration and stress occurs.

In their 1994 book, *Emergency Services Stress,* Jeffrey Mitchell and Grady Bray (1994) describe some personality characteristics of emergency services providers. They describe them as being **internally motivated**. That means that they are somewhat less motivated by external factors such as money and are more motivated by internal factors such as doing a good job. Although this makes them great emergency care providers, it sets them up for conflicts with administration, a sense that they are not appreciated by other professionals, family, or friends, and can create anxiety over their own professional competence.

Emergency services workers tend to be **action-oriented** risk takers who need to be in control. They are quick decision makers and can focus on a task under pressure. They frequently expose themselves to danger as they attempt to help others. They tackle serious situations that can expose them to disease, violent people, or dangerous environments with a calm and deliberate approach. Off duty, they often engage in highly stimulating and exciting activities because they are easily bored and enjoy staying alert. All of these add up to a stressful but exciting lifestyle.

Emergency personnel possess a strong **need-to-help** others. This trait complements the other traits in their work. It is difficult for them to say "no" to any appeal for help that they believe is legitimate. This is why frustration and stress develops when they cannot use their skills to help others who need it or when it seems that they must respond to unwarranted calls for help.

Mister Snodgrass

Panel 1: *Tuesday's Weather Forecast — Sunny and Bright, Highs in the 80's "Not a Storm Cloud in Sight."*

Panel 2: *Tuesday's Weather*

Panel 3: *Why doesn't the Sun ever listen to me?*

Finally, an intense **sense of dedication** pervades the emergency services worker. They will continue to help others even when it may be harming them. They will regularly work long hours and extra shifts. They spend their own money for extra equipment that will help them in their job. While these traits help them tackle their jobs effectively, they can also set them up for stress and isolate them from their **social support systems**: family and friends. It has been demonstrated that healthy relationships with family and friends, or a healthy social support system, can buffer some of the effects of stress. Interestingly, emergency services providers oftentimes limit their socialization to fellow workers. This is potentially a problem. When separated from the work environment due to illness or other reasons, the social support network is reduced.

OTHER STRESSORS

Ambiguity, or unpredictability, is a known stressor in many occupations. The ambiguous and unpredictable nature of emergency services work is another element in the stress equation. Waiting for the "big one," responding to unknown situations and locations, and solving bizarre and complex problems in an emergency can be stressful. Just hearing dispatch put out a call for "family violence," "unknown situation," "man down," or "multiple vehicle accident" can elicit the stress response.

Another known occupational stressor is **shift-work**. Emergency services are provided to the public "24/7"—twenty-four hours a day, seven days a week. Emergency services providers may work 8-, 12-, or 24-hour shifts. It is not uncommon to see them even work 48- to 96-hour shifts. The literature abounds with correlations between shift-work and many negative consequences (Garbarino, Beelke et al., 2002; Garbarino, De Carli et al., 2002; Karlsson, Knutsson, & Lindahl, 2001; Kitamura et al., 2002; Wilson, 2002). Shift-work has been shown to be associated with hypertension, cardiovascular disease, obesity, increased triglycerides, impaired glucose tolerance, increased sleep disorders, an increased risk of accidents, greater use of health care services, interference of social life and social problems, and increased psychological problems. Shift-work can be a great source of stress for the emergency services provider.

Other sources of occupational stress reported in the literature include conflicts with coworkers, patient care (Boudreaux et al., 1996), dealing with death, working motor vehicle accidents, fires, involvement with children (injury, illness, battery, and death reported specifically), involvement with injured persons, violent situations, use of force, and conflicts with administration.

BURNOUT

Herbert J. Freudenberger, PhD, is generally credited with coining the term *burnout*. **Burnout** is a syndrome of emotional exhaustion thought to be brought about by overwork, most frequently among individuals involved in human services occupations. It results in the progressive inability to carry out the responsibilities of one's job. Christina Maslach of the University of California, Berkeley, identified three major characteristics of the syndrome (Maslach & Jackson, 1981). The first characteristic is a progressive increase in the feeling of emotional exhaustion. Those suffering from burnout may feel "all used up" at the end of a shift. Energy seems low throughout the workday. Eventually, before even getting out of bed, the very idea of facing another day on the job feels wearisome. As emotional resources are depleted, the development of the second characteristic begins to manifest. Negative, cynical attitudes and feelings towards clients, patients, or patrons begin to permeate one's work. Those experiencing burnout begin to depersonalize people. **Depersonalization** is treating people as though they were objects. In order to protect themselves, those suffering from burnout become emotionally "hardened" and treat others callously. The third characteristic of burnout is the tendency to evaluate oneself negatively, especially when assessing their own work with those who may need their help.

Characteristics of Burnout

- Progressive increase in the feeling of emotional exhaustion.
- Negative, cynical attitudes and feelings about one's clients, patients, or patrons.
- Evaluating oneself negatively, especially when assessing the work with their patients or clients.

Originally, the idea of burnout was conceptualized as a situationally induced stress reaction. The theory is that as the quality of the work environment deteriorates or the demands of the job increase, individuals begin to experience burnout. There is no doubt that some situations, like critical incidents, become so overwhelming that even the most hardy of emergency services providers succumb to the pressures of their work. However, research indicates that personality factors may play a crucial role in stress and burnout. Piedmont (1993) demonstrated that certain personality factors were associated with higher rates of burnout. Having depressed, anxious, and antagonistic personality characteristics was predictive of burnout, despite situational influences.

Similarly, a Canadian study of paramedics found that the strongest predictor of taking mental health leave following exposure to critical incidents was also personality characteristics, not traumatic stress levels (Regehr, Goldberg, Glancy, & Knott, 2002). High egocentricity and social insecurity could account for almost 85% of the cases taking mental health leave. It is unclear whether these characteristics predispose individuals to take leave or whether the fallout of taking leave influences individuals to have increased feelings of isolation and hostility. In a population with such a high sense of dedication to their jobs, any type of leave is viewed rather cynically, even vacations. When an emergency services provider takes leave for mental health reasons, the ramifications in their social support network and at work can be devastating. Finally, a study of firefighter-paramedics demonstrated that the personality characteristics of authoritarianism and sensation-seeking were also shown to be associated with burnout (Palmer & Spaid, 1996).

The effects of burnout are potentially very serious for all involved. It can result in high job turnover, increased absenteeism, and low morale (Vettor & Kosinski, 2000). Other effects of burnout include physical exhaustion, insomnia, increased substance abuse, and marital and family problems. Burnout can lead to a decrease in the quality of care or services provided by emergency services providers. This can be particularly deleterious for such highly dedicated workers performing such vital jobs to our communities. Burnout affects the organizations, the community, providers, and their friends and family.

There is another category of stressful events for disaster and workers. These events are so powerful that they can have serious negative effects that can last the rest of their lives. They are known as critical incidents.

Key Points

- *Emergency services providers* are those who are employed or volunteer in the emergency services profession and their support staff: firefighters, EMTs, paramedics, law enforcement personnel, dispatchers, hazardous materials specialists, rescue specialists, and others.
- The term *unrealistic optimism* refers to the dichotomy exemplified by emergency services workers rating their job as more stressful compared with other occupations but also reporting their chances of being adversely affected or harmed by this stress as less than average.
- The term *environmental stressor* refers to the aspects of a particular environment that can elicit the stress response. In emergency services, this could include things such as noises at the scene, weather, hazardous materials, crowds, traffic, or violent individuals.
- Certain personality factors or traits can become stressors themselves and add to emergency services stress.
- The unpredictable nature of emergency services work and shiftwork has been identified as stressors for emergency services providers.
- *Burnout* is a syndrome of emotional exhaustion brought about by the interaction of overwork and certain personality characteristics, most frequently among individuals involved in human services occupations.
- Burnout affects organizations, the community, emergency services providers, and their friends and family.

4

Critical Incidents

OBJECTIVES

- Define critical incident.
- List common types of critical incidents.
- Recognize the occupational fatality rates of emergency services providers.
- List three common features of critical incidents.
- Define major incident.
- Recognize common reactions to critical incidents.
- Recognize some of the possible results of critical incidents.

Sometimes, emergency services providers encounter events that are more severe in impact than the everyday stressors of emergency services stress. These events have such a severe emotional and physical impact that they have the potential to overwhelm usual coping mechanisms, resulting in severe distress and impairment in the ability to cope. These traumatic events are known as **critical incidents** (Mitchell & Bray, 1994). Any event that has an unusually powerful impact on any individual emergency services worker is a critical incident. Jeffery Mitchell, PhD, coined the term *critical incident* in the 1980s and launched an international awareness of the impact of traumatic events on emergency services providers. He was instrumental in establishing the International Critical Incident Stress Foundation, Inc. (ICISF) and has been a dominant force in developing a traumatic stress intervention model for emergency service providers. He states, "... a critical incident may also be thought of as a traumatic event (i.e., an event outside the usual realm of human experience that would be markedly distressing to most individuals)" (Everly & Mitchell, 1999, p. 11). This idea is consistent with current psychotraumatology theory. The term *critical incident* could be considered an emergency services subheading under traumatic events.

At first glance, the idea that a critical incident would be distressing to almost anyone may seem somewhat arguable to some emergency services providers. Remember unrealistic optimism? Some emergency services providers mistakenly believe that when they put on their uniform, they somehow become invulnerable to the impact of stressful or traumatic events. What the definition means is that *any* event that is outside the normal experience of *any* human (not just an emergency services worker) that is a traumatic event could be a critical incident. What might be considered a traumatic event for the average person certainly has the potential to cause severe stress reactions in emergency services providers as well. Just because someone puts on a blue shirt and jumps into an emergency vehicle does not mean that person stops being a human being and suddenly become invulnerable to stress.

Other authors have joined Mitchell. Everly, Flannery, and Mitchell (1999) have described critical incidents as unexpected, time-limited, events that may involve a loss or threat to personal goals or well-being, and may represent a potential turning point in the person's life. The intensity of critical incidents often produces memories that will last a lifetime. After a critical incident, emergency services workers may ponder leaving their careers. Their relationships with friends and family may be stressed, or conversely, develop into a deeper, more meaningful experience. Critical incidents have such an impact on a person's life that they may trigger that person to pause and reexamine life and search for new or deeper meaning. Critical incidents have the potential to develop into an acute crisis and eventually PTSD (Everly & Mitchell, 1999).

EXPOSURE TO CRITICAL INCIDENTS

Some common examples of critical incidents are death or serious injury of a fellow worker in the line of duty, suicide of a fellow worker, working a scene in which a victim is known to the rescuer and is dying or in serious condition, disasters or mass casualties, excessive media coverage of an event, and death or serious injury or illness of a child (Mitchell & Bray, 1994). Any event that has an unusually powerful impact on any individual emergency services worker is a critical incident and should be handled as such.

> ### Common Types of Critical Incidents
>
> - Line of duty injury or death of a coworker
> - Suicide of a coworker
> - Incidents with victims known to the emergency services worker(s)
> - Disasters
> - Multiple casualty incidents
> - Media coverage of an event
> - Death or serious injury of a child
> - Any event that has an unusually powerful impact on personnel

Adapted from J. Mitchell and G. Bray, Emergency Services Stress: Guidelines on Preserving the Health and Careers of Emergency Services Personnel, *1st edition. © 1990. Adapted by permission of Pearson Education, Inc., Upper Saddle River, NJ.*

The ICISF and a review of the literature provide little frequency rate data for critical incidents among emergency services providers. This may be due to the ambiguous nature of the definition, the difficulty amassing this type of data, or a lack of funding and direction in this type of research. Some idea can be gleaned from existing information. One place to look is at the **prevalence** of PTSD. The American Psychiatric Association (APA) lists PTSD as a mental disorder in the *Diagnostic and Statistical Manual of Mental Disorders—IV* (DSM-IV). It lists lifetime prevalence rates ranging from 1% to 14% in the general population, with a recent study demonstrating rates of up to 25% (Hidalgo & Davidson, 2000). McFarlane's (1988) renowned Australian Ash Wednesday bushfire study of volunteer firefighters demonstrated that PTSD may have seven different patterns with varying rates. Others have reported PTSD symptomatology rates in firefighters of 9% to 17%, depending on severity of symptoms (Bryant & Harvey, 1996) with 40% reporting at least some level of psychological distress (Bryant & Harvey, 1995). Although this does not provide exposure rate data for critical incidents, it does give us some idea of impact that exposure to traumatic events is having on emergency services providers.

Another more revealing source is the national averages of occupational fatality rates. For all workers in the United States, the national average occupational fatality rate is 5.0 per 100,000 workers per year. Emergency services providers as a group have a rate that is more than twice this figure! A conscientious and meticulous study by Maguire, Hunting, Smith, and Levick (2002) calculated EMS workers' rate to be 12.7 fatalities per 100,000 annually, 14.2 for police, and 16.5 for firefighters. As a group, emergency services providers are being exposed to line of duty deaths more than twice as often as the average worker is.

Another place we can look is at the occurrence of disasters and traumatic events among the general population. Studies indicate that the prevalence of exposure to traumatic events in the general population range from 39% to almost 90% within one's lifetime, with many being exposed to more than one traumatic event (Hidalgo & Davidson, 2000; McFarlane, 1997). These rates are for the general population and emergency services providers are involved at some level with most traumatic events. Alexander and Klein (2001) report that in a six-month period, ambulance personnel report exposure to critical incidents at a rate of 82%. Another study reports that 100% of the paramedics in their sample report being exposed to at least one critical incident in the course of their careers (Regehr et al., 2002). Given this information and the nature of emergency services work, it is reasonable to conclude that the question is not so much one of prevalence, but of frequency and intensity among various populations of these workers. It is logical to assume that emergency services providers are being exposed to multiple critical incidents or traumatic events over the course of their careers.

Occupational Fatality Rates in the United States

All workers	5.0 per 100,000
EMS personnel	12.7 per 100,000
Law enforcement	14.2 per 100,000
Firefighters	16.5 per 100,000

Adapted from Annals of Emergency Medicine, 40(6), *Maguire et al., "Occupational Fatalities in Emergency Medical Services: A Hidden Crisis," 625–632, 2002, with permission from The American College of Emergency Physicians.*

COMMON FEATURES OF CRITICAL INCIDENTS

While there may be great variety in the circumstances and particulars of critical incidents, how are critical incidents the same? Werner, Bates, Bell, Murdoch, and Robinson (1992) identified three common themes or elements of critical incidents that are associated with high emotional impact on emergency services providers:

- knowing or identifying with the victim or with their family (children or young people involved; association with the victim or their family),
- large-scale incidents (multiple deaths or injuries present; goriness or enormity), and

- surprise or novelty of the incident (being unprepared or a first experience with death)

Knowing or Identifying with Victims

One of an emergency services provider's worst nightmares is to respond to a call involving friends, coworkers, or family. The shock of pulling up to a scene to find someone you know or love is simply terrible. The descriptions that emergency services providers recount about these types of scenes are painted with an array of emotions. Shock, sadness, fear, anger, guilt, and frustration seem almost like dull words compared to the intensity of emotion that these people go through. Even working an incident in which the victim(s) may simply remind an emergency worker of his or her friends or family can have devastating effects. Simple things like a child's pajamas, a woman's perfume, a familiar vehicle, a familiar face—all can cause identification with a victim and initiate a stress response. Simply hearing a familiar address come across the radio from dispatch can elicit the stress response. These types of incidents are critical incidents and should be dealt with appropriately.

Large-Scale Incidents

When people talk about large-scale, multiple-casualty incidents, certain images may come to mind. The tragic loss of the 110 people who were on board the ValueJet DC-9, Flight 592 that crashed May 11, 1996, in the Florida Everglades may come to the mind of some. Others may remember the devastating 1997 Ohio River floods. Many recall the national tragedy of the bombing of the Alfred P. Murrah Federal Building in Oklahoma City on April 19, 1997. For most of us, the terrorist attacks of September 11, 2001, will epitomize the trauma of a large-scale critical incident.

While these events were certainly large-scale, heartbreaking, mass-casualty incidents, there are countless others that impact the lives of emergency services providers that do not receive such notoriety. An event does not have to be a national news item in order for it to be a mass-casualty or major incident. A **major incident** is an event for which the available resources are insufficient to manage the number of casualties or the nature of the emergency (Sanders, 1994). Therefore, a multiple-casualty automobile accident can be a major incident for a small service. When law enforcement calls for backup, air transport is utilized, a multiple-alarm fire call goes out—all of these are potential critical incidents. Not all major incidents are critical incidents and not all critical incidents are major incidents.

However, if the number of emergency services workers and available equipment is having difficulty meeting the demands of an incident, then stress is probably high and a critical incident could be taking place. All major incidents should be considered potential critical incidents.

Surprise or Novelty

Most emergency services personnel recognize that when new or inexperienced personnel are faced with death for the first time, stress may be high. However, not everyone recognizes that when an incident occurs for which personnel or a service is unprepared, or when personnel have to improvise because of unusual circumstances, stress is also inevitable. It can sometimes be difficult to admit that we were unprepared for something. When we consider the personality characteristics of emergency services workers and the phenomenon of unrealistic optimism, it is not surprising that emergency services workers have an even harder time dealing with unusual events for which they may not be fully prepared. When spontaneous or surprising events are ignored or denied, how will it be feasible to recognize the impact that an event is having on personnel? It is impractical and possibly even dangerous to ignore the impact a critical incident may be having. It is unreasonable to expect that a service or any individual can *always* be prepared for *every* incident. This is fallacious reasoning. Just because some or all personnel at a scene are "seasoned" or veterans, does not mean that a critical incident has not occurred and that personnel are not impacted by it.

REACTIONS TO CRITICAL INCIDENTS

Just as our reactions to someone pulling out in front of us in traffic are normal, so too are the reactions to critical incidents. Reactions to stressful events are not a sign of weakness, failure, or mental illness. They are signs that normal, caring people have been exposed to an unusual and oftentimes, tragic event. Nixon, Schorr, Boudreaux, & Vincent (1999) report on the reactions of Oklahoma City firefighters in a study following the bombing of the Alfred P. Murrah Federal Building. They found that 64% of the respondents reported moderate to severe effects from the bombing. Not surprisingly, a further 12% could not even label the severity of the event.

The common signs and symptoms of acute or delayed stress following critical incidents fall into the same four categories as ordinary stress: physical, cognitive, affective, and behavioral (Mitchell & Bray,

1994). Some of the reactions are very similar. The major difference may be the intensity, frequency, or interference these reactions cause. Some reactions to critical incidents may be so intense or severe that immediate medical care is necessary. Other reactions, while still serious, do not require emergency treatment but may require intervention, nonetheless.

Signs and Symptoms Requiring Immediate Corrective Action

PHYSICAL

Chest pain*
Difficulty breathing*
Excessive blood pressure*
Collapse from exhaustion*
Cardiac arrhythmias*
Signs of severe shock*
Excessive dehydration*
Dizziness*
Excessive vomiting*
Blood in stool*

EMOTIONAL

Panic reactions
Shock-like state
Phobic reaction
General loss of control
Inappropriate emotions

COGNITIVE

Decreased alertness to surroundings
Difficulties making decisions
Hyperalertness
Generalized mental confusion
Disorientation to person, place, time
Serious disruption in thinking
Seriously slowed thinking
Problems in naming familiar items
Problem recognizing familiar people

BEHAVIORAL

Significant change in speech patterns
Excessively angry outbursts
Crying spells
Antisocial acts (e.g., violence)
Extreme hyperactivity

*Indicates a need for medical evaluation.

Source: J. Mitchell and G. Bray, *Emergency Services Stress: Guidelines on Preserving the Health and Careers of Emergency Services Personnel, 1st edition.* © 1990. Reprinted by permission of Pearson Education, Inc., Upper Saddle River, NJ.

Because of varying reactions to critical incidents, diverse levels of current or ongoing stressors in workers' lives, an assortment of learned coping or survival skills, and personality factors, it is difficult to know who is most vulnerable to critical incident stress. After a critical incident, a downward spiral toward severe depression, hopelessness, and isolation has been documented. Sometimes, this spiral is temporarily blocked with coping mechanisms and resurfaces as long as 2 to 3 years later or more. Critical incident stress can result in substance abuse, depression, divorce, loss of employment, illnesses, PTSD, and even suicide. Managing the traumatic and potentially life-changing aftermath of critical incidents is vital.

Signs and Symptoms Not Requiring Immediate Corrective Action

PHYSICAL

Nausea	Rapid heart rate
Upset stomach	Muscle aches
Tremors (lips, hands)	Sleep disturbances
Feeling uncoordinated	Dry mouth
Profuse sweating	Shakes
Chills	Vision problems
Diarrhea	Fatigue

COGNITIVE

Confusion	Blaming someone
Lowered attention span	Distressing dreams
Calculation difficulties	Disruption in logical thinking
Memory problems	
Poor concentration	
Seeing an event over and over	

EMOTIONAL

Anticipatory anxiety	Feeling lost
Denial	Feeling abandoned
Fear	Worried
Survivor guilt	Wishing to hide
Uncertainty of feelings	Wishing to die
Depression	Anger
Grief	Feeling numb
Feeling hopeless	Identifying with the victim
Feeling overwhelmed	

BEHAVIORAL

Change in activity	Increased smoking
Withdrawal	Increased alcohol intake
Suspiciousness	Overly vigilant to environment
Change in communications	Excessive humor
Change in interactions with others	Excessive silence
Increased or decreased food intake	Unusual behavior

Source: J. Mitchell and G. Bray, *Emergency Services Stress: Guidelines on Preserving the Health and Careers of Emergency Services Personnel, 1st edition.* © 1990. Reprinted by permission of Pearson Education, Inc., Upper Saddle River, NJ.

Key Points

- The term *critical incident* refers to events that have the potential to overwhelm usual coping mechanisms, resulting in severe distress in most individuals.
- Universal examples of critical incidents are death or serious injury of a fellow worker in the line of duty, suicide of a fellow worker, working on a person who is known to the rescuer and is dying or in serious condition, disasters or mass casualties, excessive media coverage of an event, and death or serious injury or illness of a child.
- Three common themes of critical incidents that are associated with high emotional impact on emergency services workers are knowing or identifying with the victim, large-scale incidents, and surprise or novelty of the incident.
- The common signs and symptoms of acute or delayed stress following critical incidents fall into four categories: physical, cognitive, affective, and behavioral.

5

Posttraumatic Stress Disorder

OBJECTIVES

- Identify past terms for PTSD.
- Trace the development of the PTSD criteria.
- Identify Criterion A of the current diagnostic criteria for PTSD.
- List the three other major criteria (B, C, and D) for PTSD.
- Identify the length of time symptoms must be present for diagnosis of PTSD.
- Differentiate between ASD and PTSD.
- Recognize Criterion F of the current diagnostic criteria for PTSD.
- Identify the personality trait of neuroticism (N) that is correlated with traumatic symptomology.

Most people will experience a traumatic event at some point in their life. The 1996 Detroit Area Survey of Trauma reported a lifetime prevalence rate of traumatic exposure of nearly 90% (as cited in Hidalgo & Davidson, 2000), and lifetime prevalence rates of posttraumatic stress disorder (PTSD) in "the general population seems to be around 8% to 9%, with women having a higher risk for PTSD than men" (Hidalgo & Davidson, 2000, p. 7). As mentioned in chapter 4, the APA lists PTSD as a mental disorder in the DSM-IV (American Psychiatric Association, 1994). It cites community-based studies revealing lifetime prevalence rates ranging from 1% to 14% in the general population.

After the bombing of the Alfred P. Murrah Federal Building in Oklahoma City, firefighters who worked the disaster were compared with primary victims (North et al., 2002). The prevalence of PTSD related to the bombing was significantly lower in the firefighters compared to primary victims, 13% and 23%, respectively. The firefighters' prevalence rate was within the prevalence rate of 1% to 14% reported in the DSM-IV (American Psychiatric Association, 1994). On the other hand, another study of firefighters reported on the prevalence of posttraumatic stress as well. It reported that 40% of the sample reported some degree of psychological distress, 37% reported posttraumatic stress symptoms, and 24% reported posttraumatic stress (Bryant & Harvey, 1995).

Traumatic exposure and PTSD have the potential to devastate a person. Research has shown that traumatic exposure and PTSD can have a serious impact on a person's health and functioning (Bisson, 1997; Bryant & Harvey, 1995, 1996; Everly, 1996; Friedman, 1996; Gold et al., 2000; Harris, Baloğlu, & Stacks, 2002; Hidalgo & Davidson, 2000; McFarlane, 1988, 1997; Regehr et al., 2002; Saigh & Bremner, 1999; Wilson, 1996; Young, 2000). This in turn causes pain, confusion, and life-altering adversities to those most close to the individual. The cluster of symptoms that define PTSD can be so devastating to an individual that it results in substance abuse, depression, divorce, loss of employment, illnesses, and even death, most often as a result of suicide. Additionally, it has a considerable economic burden on not only the individual and those most close to him, but also on the health care system and society as a whole (Hidalgo & Davidson, 2000). Since this life-changing disorder has such overwhelming potential for emergency services workers, their families, friends, and coworkers, it is worthwhile to review its history and the current diagnostic criteria.

HISTORICAL EVOLUTION OF THE DIAGNOSTIC CRITERIA OF PTSD

Although descriptions of posttraumatic stress reactions are cited as far back as the sixth century BC (Everly, 1996), it has only been since 1980 that the APA listed PTSD as a mental disorder in the *Diagnostic and Statistical Manual of Mental Disorders*—III (DSM-III). Before that time, the cluster of PTSD-like symptoms has had many names. During the 1860s it was called *railway spine* since symptoms were believed to have been caused by injury to neurons secondary to collisions or other traumas. During the American Civil War, it was called *soldiers' irritable heart* or "Da Costa's syndrome." Kraepelin, the nineteenth-century

German nosologist (one who studies and classifies diseases), termed the symptoms *schreckneurose,* meaning "fright neuroses." During World War I, it was referred to as *shell shock.* In 1943, Alfred Adler made reference to the *post-traumatic mental complications* of the survivors of the notorious Boston's Coconut Grove nightclub fire. In 1945, Grinker and Spiegel described the serious symptoms of a B-24 gunner with *combat neuroses.* From the Vietnam War we saw the terms *neuropsychiatric casualties* and *delayed stress response syndrome* (in Saigh & Bremner, 1999). Sigmund Freud, with his career-launching publication of *Studies in Hysteria* with Josef Breuer in 1895, developed a paradigm of PTSD-like neurosis (Wilson, 1996). This and other writings by Freud illustrate a remarkable understanding of posttraumatic stress and the limitations explaining it completely under his model. Other terms like *battle fatigue, rape trauma syndrome, gross stress reaction,* and *traumatic neurosis* have referred to the cluster of symptoms that today we call PTSD.

The modern biological approaches of psychotraumatology were stimulated by research on World War I veterans during the 1940s by Abram Kardiner (Friedman, 1996), and his book, *The Traumatic Neuroses of War,* is cited as the source of the DSM-III criteria for PTSD (in Young, 2000). Since Freud, the historical evolution of the diagnostic criteria of PTSD has seen the convergence of neuroscience, experimental psychology, clinical psychiatry, and sociology. Although it is beyond this text to review the many theories of traumatic stress, it is worthwhile to examine fundamental developments and changes that have influenced the evolution of the current diagnostic criteria for PTSD.

Past Terms for PTSD

- Soldiers' irritable heart, or Da Costa's syndrome
- Schreckneurose, or fright neuroses
- Shell shock
- Post-traumatic mental complications
- Combat neuroses
- Neuropsychiatric casualties
- Battle fatigue
- Rape trauma syndrome
- Gross stress reaction
- Traumatic neurosis

DSM-I

In 1952, thirteen years after Sigmund Freud's death, the APA published its first *Diagnostic and Statistical Manual of Mental Disorders.* Known today as the DSM-I, it contained the category **Gross Stress Reaction** (GSR) that is the underpinnings of the current PTSD criteria. Influenced by Freud's thinking about traumatic neurosis, GSR was described as occurring to "more or less 'normal' persons who have experienced intolerable stress." However, there were some illustrations that differ from our current understanding of PTSD. GSR was placed in a transient situational personality disorders category. Such conditions were expected to resolve quickly. PTSD as we know it today can be diagnosed years after exposure and can be a chronic condition. Prolonged or persistent reactions were classified in another category that implied the possibility of a **premorbid** (existing prior to the onset of the current symptoms or illness) condition such as psychosis, neurosis, and character disorders. When referring to GSR, the DSM-I stated that "when promptly treated, the condition may clear rapidly," reflecting the assumption that rapid intervention facilitated recovery. It divided precipitating stressors of GSR into two categories, stating that "the particular stress involved will be specified as: 1). combat or, 2). civilian catastrophe" (American Psychiatric Association, 1980).

The DSM-I established a fundamental understanding of traumatic stress when it specified "conditions of great or unusual stress" that occur to "more or less normal persons."

DSM-II

The DSM-II introduced the classification of *transient situational disturbance* (in Saigh & Bremner, 1999). It was published in 1968 after a time in history in which there were all kinds of traumatic events worldwide: the Korean and Vietnam wars, colonial wars and revolutions, the assassination of John F. Kennedy, civil violence in Northern Ireland, wars in the Middle East, major natural disasters in many parts of the world, and recognition of the prevalence of childhood sexual abuse (Wilson, 1996). These events and various traumatized populations were being investigated, researched, and extensively published in medical and scientific journals of the time (Wilson, 1996). Individual researchers were using a wide range of competing terms to describe the same phenomenon, and this seemed to be creating more confusion rather than coherence (Saigh & Bremner, 1999). Because of this, questions were raised regarding the simplicity and inadequacies of the DSM-II criteria. Still referred to as GSR, the disorder was placed into the category Adjustment Reaction of Adult Life, and provided three short illustrations. In an appendix, it listed a cumbersome list of examples of stressful life events. Considered woefully short of the mark by many, the advent of the DSM-III criteria seemed inevitable.

DSM-III

With the publication of the DSM-III in 1980, the name for PTSD was born. A Reactive Disorders Committee drew on their clinical experience and the existing literature to formulate the diagnostic criteria forming PTSD (Saigh & Bremner, 1999). PTSD was placed among the anxiety disorders and four criteria were provided. In order to receive a diagnosis of PTSD, an individual had to manifest a mandatory exposure to extreme stress (Criterion A). In addition, the presence of at least four symptoms from three cluster groups of symptoms (listed as Criteria B, C, and D) also had to be present. One of the most notable advances over previous DSM classifications was the prime criterion for PTSD: the "existence of a recognizable stressor that would evoke significant symptoms of distress in almost everyone." This provided researchers an opportunity to advance the idea of normal humans experiencing abnormally stressful events (Wilson, 1996) and served as an acknowledgment that divergent stressors (such as sexual assault, war-related events, serious accidents, or disasters) could induce these symptoms. Recognition of horrors such as intrusive thoughts and dreams, reexperiences of the precipitating event or **flashbacks**, numbing, guilt, and cognitive difficulties were among the symptoms allowing a continuum of symptom severity and pathological impact.

There was opposition to the DSM-III PTSD classification (Young, 2000). Many doubted the validity of the principles establishing the new criteria as unscientific. They believed that what was now being called PTSD was simply the cooccurrence of already established classifications, most notably depression, generalized anxiety disorder, and panic disorder. The Reactive Disorders Committee was believed to be internally influenced by a group of psychiatrists sympathetic to the plight of many Vietnam War veterans, and that they worked to create a classification not necessarily based on the theory and scientific understanding of the time, but on the bureaucratic system of the Veterans Administration and a commitment to ending the victimization of certain veterans (Young, 2000). This meant establishing a classification that did not involve preexisting conditions and that could be easily service connected.

DSM-III-R

Revisions to the DSM-III began almost as soon as it was published. Initial research began in 1983 and the final efforts were published in 1987 as the DSM-III-R. It attempted to clarify language, meaning, and the specificity of reactions to trauma (Wilson, 1996). The mandatory Criterion A was reworded to become more inclusive, stating that the precipitating event could now be any "event that is outside the range of usual human experience that would be markedly distressing to almost anyone" (American Psychiatric Association, 1987). In addition, the DSM-III-R now explicitly demarcated the nightmarish Criteria B, C, and D:

- *Criterion B:* Persistent reexperience of the traumatic event (such as dreams and flashbacks).
- *Criterion C:* Avoidance or numbing behaviors (such as avoiding activities associated with the event or feeling detached).
- *Criterion D:* Persistent symptoms of arousal (such as difficulty falling asleep or irritability).

The symptoms listed under the criteria had to be associated to the traumatic event and could not be present before it.

CURRENT UNDERSTANDING OF PTSD

The DSM-III and DSM-III-R spawned a significant amount of scientific research that helped influence further development of the criteria. This research was reviewed and a number of clinical trials were specifically employed to refine the criteria (Saigh & Bremner, 1999). These new criteria are used as the root of our understanding of PTSD today.

DSM-IV

Although relatively minor changes were made between the DSM-III-R and the DSM-IV, one change in the definition of a traumatic event is noteworthy. Criterion A is now two-pronged, indicating that the person must have experienced or witnessed a life-threatening event *and* responded to it with fear, horror, or helplessness (American Psychiatric Association, 1994). Expanding examples of traumatic events, it also made reference to youth and "inappropriate sexually traumatic events without threatened or actual violence." Even receiving *news* about stressful events is understood to be an avenue of traumatization. Currently, the model holds that just observing certain events are traumatic and potential precipitators of PTSD. The other three major criteria remained essentially the same: persistent reexperience of the event (Criterion B), avoidance and numbing (Criterion C), and increased arousal (Criterion D). A new Criterion E requires that symptom duration be at least one month. This differentiates it from a new category,

Acute Stress Disorder (ASD). The most distinguishing difference between the two is time. ASD lasts for at least two days and does not persist beyond four weeks after the traumatic event.

The DSM-IV also added a Criterion F that maintains the disorder must cause "clinically significant distress or impairment in social, occupational, or other important areas of functioning." It is not enough to have the symptoms. The symptoms must cause a level of suffering that interferes with a person's life. It is hard to imagine otherwise. The nightmares, constant intrusive thoughts, flashbacks, isolation, difficulty sleeping, and other symptoms would be distressful to anyone. The misery caused by these symptoms disrupts the ability to work, play, and relate with others. Finally, the current criteria also define three "specifiers" of PTSD: Acute, Chronic, and With Delayed Onset. For a more complete listing of the DSM-IV criteria for ASD and PTSD, see appendix A.

Abbreviated Diagnostic Criteria for PTSD

- Exposure to a traumatic event *and* a response of fear, horror, or helplessness.
- Persistent reexperiences of the traumatic event.
- Persistent avoidance of stimuli associated with the trauma and numbing.
- Persistent symptoms of increased arousal.
- Duration of more than one month.
- The disturbance causes clinically significant distress or impairment in social, occupational, or other important areas of functioning.

For a more complete listing of the DSM-IV's diagnostic criteria, see appendix A.

Adapted with permission from the Diagnostic and Statistical Manual of Mental Disorders, *Text Revision, Copyright 2000. American Psychiatric Association.*

Personality and Trauma

Simply being exposed to a traumatic event is not enough to trigger PTSD. In other words, just because someone is exposed to a traumatic event does not mean that they are going to necessarily develop PTSD. Researchers have tried to understand what other variables may be correlated with PTSD besides exposure. Personality traits may account for reactions to traumatic events more than would first be assumed. General personality research has converged on the existence of five major factors of personality: neuroticism or negative affectivity (N), extraversion (E), openness to experience (O), agreeableness (A), and conscientiousness (C) (Costa & McCrae, 1997; McCrae & Costa, 1997; McCrae & Oliver, 1992). Although some variations in naming and identifying the individual factors exist, the Five-Factor Model (FFM) is well accepted and provides a common language and framework for the organization of research and assessment of individuals (McCrae & Oliver, 1992).

Since the establishment of the DSM-IV classification of PTSD, the association between the neuroticism factor (N) and traumatic stress has been increasingly implicated. Using a variation of the FFM, negativism and psychopathology traits were second only to traumatic exposure in predicting PTSD symptom severity in a military peacekeeping sample (Bramsen & Dirkzwager, 2000). In a study of emergency services personnel and highway workers exposed to an earthquake disaster, the best predictor of symptomatic distress on four different measures was the Adjustment scale of the Hogan Personality Inventory, which is empirically related to the neuroticism (N) factor of the FFM (Weiss, Marmar, Metzler, & Ronfeldt, 1995).

Neuroticism, anxiety, depression, and excitement seeking were found to be significantly associated with emotional exhaustion. McFarlane and colleagues (1988) followed a group of Australian firefighters ($n = 469$) who were responsible for battling the Australian Ash Wednesday bushfire disaster. They reported that predisaster neuroticism (N), avoidant coping, and history of prior mental health treatment were more predictive of chronic symptoms than was exposure to the critical incident. In addition, police officers with lower levels of cynicism, pessimism, neuroticism, perfectionism, and higher levels of hardiness may be less susceptible to perceived stress than are peers with inverse levels of these characteristics (Anshel, 2000). Alexander and Klein (2001) also found that ambulance personnel with "hardy" personalities display significantly less PTSD symptomatology. However, they raise an important issue; personality features that may protect emergency services personnel from stress and traumatic stress may not necessarily be the features that are best suited for the performance of emergency services. So, it seems that the neuroticism factor (N) of personality, "hardiness," coping styles, and prior mental health treatment may be more reliable predictors of posttraumatic symptom risk than simply exposure alone.

CLOSING

What is defined or identified as PTSD today has been known by many names throughout history. The criteria first established by the APA in 1952 have evolved over the last fifty or so years giving psychology a much better understanding of psychotraumatology and PTSD. What this model describes are horrors that bring fear, distress, isolation, and a sense of hopelessness to a large number of people. Treatment modalities reported in the literature range from "metatherapeutic" or neurocognitive approaches to neurophysiological psychology. A rich and diversified amount of research on PTSD from many disciplines, including integrated approaches, fills the scientific literature. Even though the DSM-IV criteria are well accepted, there are already new discoveries and thoughts about PTSD that plead for future research and development that is more systematic (Wilson, 1996).

Many people try to prevent a traumatic experience from further developing into something as life changing as PTSD. CISM is an integrated and comprehensive multicomponent program designed to help mitigate the impact of traumatic events and prevent PTSD. This system, CISM, is the focus of the next chapter.

Key Points

- PTSD has been known by many names and its history dates back to the sixth century.
- With the publication of the DSM-III in 1980, the name for PTSD was born.
- One of the most notable advances of the DSM-III was the prime criterion for PTSD: the "existence of a recognizable stressor that would evoke significant symptoms of distress in almost everyone."
- The DSM-III-R reworded Criterion A to become more inclusive, stating that the precipitating event could now be any "event that is outside the range of usual human experience that would be markedly distressing to almost anyone."
- The DSM-IV defined a traumatic event as a two-pronged criterion, indicating that the person must have experienced or witnessed a life-threatening event *and* responded to it with fear, horror, or helplessness.
- Even receiving *news* about stressful events is understood to be an avenue of traumatization.
- Personality traits, especially the neuroticism factor (N), may account for reactions to traumatic events more than would first be assumed.

6

Critical Incident Stress Management

OBJECTIVES

- Define CISM.
- Recognize the seven core elements of CISM.
- Describe how individuals and organizations prepare for stress and critical incidents.
- Define and describe demobilization.
- Define and describe defusing.
- Define and describe CISD.
- List the seven phases of a CISD.
- Define PD.
- Define process.
- Describe how PD and CISD are different.
- Recognize the goals of CISD and PD.
- Identify the rules of a CISD.
- Define primary, secondary, and tertiary victims.
- Recognize examples of direct and indirect impact of trauma on families of emergency services providers.
- Recognize reasons for referral to professional mental health services.

Since its inception almost twenty years ago by Jeffery Mitchell, PhD, CISM has evolved and grown into a comprehensive program. It evolved out of earlier crisis intervention and group psychological debriefing techniques (Everly, 1995; Everly et al., 1999). A network of hundreds of CISM teams has developed in the United States, Canada, Australia, and Western Europe. Because of this, CISM is considered a standard of care in crisis intervention for victims of critical incidents and its extensive utilization is widely cited in the professional literature (Bisson, 1997; Dyregrov, 1997; Everly, 1995; Jenkins, 1996; Neely & Spitzer, 1997; Raphael & Meldrum, 1995). **CISM** can be defined as an integrated and comprehensive multicomponent program for the provision of crisis and disaster mental health service for emergency services providers (Everly & Mitchell, 1999).

CORE ELEMENTS OF CISM

Initially, CISDs were the focus of CISM. At the outset, CISD was somewhat synonymous with CISM. This concept has since evolved. CISM consists of much more than just a debriefing. CISM now denotes a collection of crisis interventions and technologies for stress preparation and prevention, as well as individual and group interventions. CISD is just one part of CISM. CISM has internationally flourished and has evolved into seven core-integrated elements or services (Everly & Mitchell, 1999).

Teams are usually comprised of volunteers, although some teams and individuals charge for services. Volunteer teams typically offer these services free of charge or ask for donations or reimbursement of expenses. Teams are comprised of specially trained peer members (usually emergency services providers, nurses, and others) and mental health professionals.

The Seven Core Elements of CISM

- Precrisis preparation
- Demobilization procedures
- Individual acute crisis counseling
- Defusings
- CISDs
- Family crisis intervention
- Follow-up procedures and referrals

A more detailed table of the elements may be found in appendix C.

Adapted from Aggression and Violent Behavior, 5(1), *Everly et al., "Critical Incident Stress Management (CISM): A Review of the Literature," 23–40, Copyright 1999, with permission from Elsevier and from* Critical Incident Stress Management, 2nd edition, *Everly and Mitchell, Copyright 1999, with permission from Chevron Publishing.*

International Critical Incident Stress Foundation, Inc. The majority of CISM teams belong to a loosely associated network facilitated by the International Critical Incident Stress Foundation, Inc. (ICISF). Contact information for the foundation can be found in appendix D.

Precrisis Preparation

Precrisis preparations for emergency services organizations and individuals establish and clarify expectations about critical incidents, improve coping skills, and provide information about CISM. This usually takes the form of meetings or training sessions with organizations and families, but can include assisting with the development of procedures and protocols, disaster drills, conferences, and other forums. Other preparations include stress management lectures and organizational meetings about stress and critical incident stress issues. CISM teams themselves also prepare through additional training sessions, continuing education, meetings, networking, and case reviews.

Demobilization Procedures

A demobilization is a group intervention used behind the lines at large-scale incidents to facilitate emergency services workers' transition away from the scene. A structured demobilization area is set up to provide food, rest, and information about traumatic stress and the further support that will be available in the days and weeks following the incident. It is conducted by the CISM team members using established procedures. The process usually takes about 30 minutes. After a demobilization, crews are then typically released to off-duty status.

Individual Acute Crisis Counseling

Known as **"one-on-ones,"** individual acute crisis counseling is usually provided on-scene by trained peers or mental health CISM team members. However, sometimes one-on-ones occur spontaneously away from scenes when individuals may feel more comfortable engaging with team members about critical incidents. One-on-ones have been conducted on scenes, in emergency rooms after transport of patients, at stations, in offices, or even (rarely) over the telephone. The goals of one-on-ones are to mitigate the acute stress of the individual and to facilitate access to other interventions.

Defusings

A **defusing** is a flexible, small group discussion of a critical incident usually conducted within 12 hours of the event. A crew is taken out of service and often meets back at the station or other suitable location. Defusings last about 30–45 minutes and are often conducted by a peer team member. As a shorter, more flexible version of a CISD (see below), the goals are to smooth the progress of returning to service or to off-duty status, stabilize the working crew, reduce tension, and teach basic concepts of stress and stress management. It *may* eliminate the need for a formal debriefing, but unlike CISD, the defusing is not necessarily designed to achieve closure of a critical incident. A defusing has three phases: Introduction Phase, Exploration Phase, and Information Phase.

Critical Incident Stress Debriefing

The most popular element utilized by emergency services personnel after a critical incident is a **critical incident stress debriefing (CISD).** CISD is also known as the "Mitchell model." CISD is a seven-stage group crisis intervention technique. This formal, structured group meeting emphasizes discussion of the facts surrounding the critical incident (informational elements), ventilation of emotions, normalization of reactions, and stress management education. Mitchell states that the educational and informational elements are of great assistance for emergency personnel in understanding and dealing with the stress generated by the critical incident. The seven phases or stages proceed as follows: introduction, fact, thought, reaction, symptom, teaching, and reentry phases (see appendix B for a more complete description of each phase). The intervention is recommended to be a one-time intervention that takes place at least 24 hours post-incident. It is generally conducted within ten days and as late as three to four weeks after a critical incident.

The CISD Process

- Introduction Phase
- Fact Phase
- Thought Phase
- Reaction Phase
- Symptom Phase
- Teaching Phase
- Reentry Phase

For a more detailed explanation of the phases, see appendix B.

Adapted from Critical Incident Stress Management, 2nd edition, *Everly and Mitchell, Copyright 1999, with permission from Chevron Publishing.*

Process Debriefing

Atle Dyregrov coined the term **process debriefings** (PD) utilizing a format similar to the Mitchell-model (Dyregrov, 1997, 1999). In process debriefings, a greater emphasis is placed on the leader of the group and what is known as *process*. In psychology, **process** is a term that flourishes in interactional psychology. It refers to the communication and the nature of the relationship between people. It emphasizes the *how* and *why* something is said as opposed to the content of what is said. For example, in a debriefing concerning the near-death of a fellow worker, one of the participants said, "I had to take out the AED [automatic external defibrillator] and shock him. I *had* to shock him!" The content is about what any provider would have to do. The *process* is relaying to the listeners a much greater depth about the experience of having to defibrillate someone you work, play, and live with for 24 hours at a time. Being a rescuer at the near-death of someone you know well is unexpected and traumatic. These process issues during a debriefing typically impact the entire group and the leader guides the group through these issues.

PD, then, places a greater emphasis on putting thoughts and emotions into words and recognizing how that impacts the group. Because PD places more emphasis on process, it takes longer. Whereas CISD is designed to take 1–1.5 hours, PD can take 3–3.5 hours. When recognized, process issues add golden opportunities to increase group cohesiveness or redirect away from personal issues back to group issues. The leader plays an important role in making this happen.

Another major difference between CISD and PD is the environment. In CISD, participants sit in an unobstructed circle. In PD, participants sit in a rectangular format at tables with the team leader sitting in a visible, authoritarian position. Although this may not seem important to some, physical environment plays an important role in setting the type of atmosphere desired. PD also sets clear limits on the number of participants to fifteen or less. CISD is designed for use with even larger groups. PD also places an emphasis on the nature of the group and obstacles to group process.

Goals of CISD/PD. The goals of CISD have been expressed in several ways over the years. Early in its development, the goal of CISD was to reduce the impact of critical incidents and to accelerate the recovery of normal people who are suffering through normal but painful reactions to abnormal events. Mitchell coined the phrase "to mitigate the impact of critical incidents," and has used it extensively in text and lectures around the country. Research echoes this goal, adding the prevention of PTSD (Everly, 1996) and the identification of those who may need more intensive, psychological support.

In a review of the literature, Everly et al. (1999) state that the goals of CISD are to prevent maladaptive responses to critical incidents and to utilize group format as opposed to individual intervention. More recently, the goals have been described in terms that are more clinical. In their most recent text, Everly and Mitchell (1999) state that the goals of CISD are to mitigate the adverse psychological impact of a traumatic event by reducing the intensity and chronicity of symptoms subsequent to the trauma. Interestingly, the introduction of a new goal—that CISD is also to bring or facilitate "psychological closure" to a traumatic event—has been added to the list.

For Dyregrov, the aims of PD are to prevent unnecessary aftereffects, accelerate normal recovery, stimulate group cohesion (in work groups or natural groups), normalize reactions, stimulate emotional ventilation, and promote a cognitive "grip" on the situation (Dyregrov, 1997). These goals and the claims surrounding them have been the focus of critics of CISM and CISD/PD (see chapter 7).

Confidentiality and Rules Surrounding CISD. Debriefings (both PD and CISD) are highly confidential, structured discussions about what happened, and they examine how the critical incident is impacting personnel. This means that no recordings are allowed, no notes are taken, and participants agree to guard the debriefing as confidential. A report may be submitted by the team that does not name personnel or what they said. A team's report usually only documents the number of participants, types of services involved, the debriefers' names, and other statistical data.

Personnel who were not on-scene, such as family, friends, and the news media, are not allowed entry into the debriefing. If those groups have become victims, separate debriefings or other appropriate interventions may be conducted especially for them. Participants in a CISD can be assured that what is said there stays there. There are no breaks during a CISD. If someone leaves, a team member will follow him or her out to ensure their well-being and possibly spend a short time with them one-on-one with the goal of bringing the participant back into the debriefing. Personnel are requested to be off-duty and will be asked to turn off radios, pagers, and cell phones in order to keep a very serious process uninterrupted by distractions. Although personnel are not required to speak, by sharing one's perspective, others are able to see a bigger picture that they might not have seen otherwise. In addition, as described in the first chapter on the nature of stress, talking and processing about stressful events is a major stress management technique that is highly effective.

Debriefing Rules

- Strict confidentiality
- CISD is a formal discussion, not a critique
- No family, friends, or news media are allowed
- No breaks
- Personnel are requested to be off duty
- Radios, pagers, mobile phones, and other distractions are to be turned off or set to vibrate or silent mode.
- Though not required to share, participation is highly encouraged
- No rank during the CISD (supervisors and administration may wish to have a separate CISD)
- No leaving during a CISD
- No food, drink, or tobacco products

Adapted from Aggression and Violent Behavior, 5(1), *Everly et al., "Critical Incident Stress Management (CISM): A Review of the Literature," 23–40, Copyright 1999, with permission from Elsevier and from* Critical Incident Stress Management, 2nd edition, *Everly and Mitchell, Copyright 1999, with permission from Chevron Publishing.*

Family Crisis Intervention

Families and significant others of emergency services workers are a group of very important people who are affected by the tragedy of critical incidents and the stress of daily emergency services work. When we discuss victims of critical incidents, we speak of primary victims, secondary victims, and tertiary victims. **Primary victims** are those people directly involved in an incident: patients and witnesses. Emergency services workers are considered **secondary victims.** Families and significant others are often forgotten when it comes to formal interventions. They are considered **tertiary victims** of critical incidents.

When families and significant others in the lives of emergency services workers know or suspect that their loved one is on-scene of a critical incident, they are affected by media reports and conversations with others. They worry about their safety and well-being. They may even see them on television news reports. They anxiously await

Families are impacted by critical incidents as tertiary victims.

the safe return of their loved one so that they may be there to support them and hear about the incident.

Whether there was media coverage or not, when the emergency services worker returns home from a critical incident, he has been affected by the tragedy. The impact of the crisis now spreads to family members and significant others either directly, indirectly, or both (Everly & Mitchell, 1999).

Direct impact on families and significant others can take the form of abuse, abandonment, violence, or neglect. The rage, frustration, and helplessness the emergency services worker is grappling with can be displaced to those who are cared about most. This is similar to the old "kick-the-dog syndrome," except the targets are people in close relationships. They may not even be aware that it is happening, only that something is wrong and that they hurt.

Some emergency workers return home, and isolate themselves and withdraw after a critical incident. They may self-medicate with alcohol or other substances. They may become irritable and argumentative to keep family members from getting too close. They may inappropriately withdraw to chores or hobbies for long periods to avoid contact with family members. These types of behavior affect the family and significant others of emergency services workers and is known as **indirect impact.**

CISM family programs allow organizations to extend their investments in their employees to include the employee's family and significant others. Most programs rely heavily on preincident education. Pre-education helps families to understand the stressors and normal reactions to critical incidents, identifies positive and negative coping strategies, and encourages the development of survival skills. Discussions about cumulative stress and long-term coping strategies are also a part of pre-educational sessions. Following critical incidents, it may be very appropriate to have specialized, family-oriented debriefings.

Follow-Ups and Referrals

Many emergency services workers hesitate to seek out existing traditional employee assistance or mental health services because of fears of appearing "weak" or as failures, or because of fears of documentation ending up in their employee file. Herein lies one of the great benefits of CISM. CISM programs ensure that all the emergency services workers involved in a critical incident have the opportunity for support. During the interventions, emergency services workers who may need further follow-up can be identified. They can be provided the resources and encouragement that may be essential to initiating the help they need.

> ### Selected Reasons for Referrals
>
> - Psychological and/or psychiatric services
> - Medical services
> - Religious or spiritual services
> - Family support services
> - Financial aid services
> - Career counseling
> - Legal services

Adapted from Critical Incident Stress Management, 2nd edition, *Everly and Mitchell, Copyright 1999, with permission from Chevron Publishing.*

Two to three weeks after a debriefing or other intervention, a team member may follow-up with a contact person to assess the status of participants and inquire about any other needs. Sometimes, with large events, the one-year anniversary date may revive past memories and feelings. Follow-ups, special interventions, and/or services are often implemented.

CISM has come a long way in the past twenty years. However, critiques, controversies, and discussions in the literature continue. In the next chapter, we explore some of those issues.

Key Points

- *CISM* can be defined as an integrated and comprehensive multi-component program for the provision of crisis and disaster mental health services that has evolved into seven core elements.
- *Precrisis preparations* for emergency services organizations and individuals establish and clarify expectations about critical incidents, improve coping skills, and provide information about stress and CISM.
- *One-on-ones* are individual acute crisis counseling sessions provided to an emergency services provider and is usually provided on-scene by trained peers or mental health CISM team members.
- A *demobilization* is a group intervention used behind the lines at large-scale incidents to facilitate emergency services workers' transition away from the scene.
- A *defusing* is a flexible, small group discussion of a critical incident usually conducted within 12 hours of a traumatic event.
- *CISD* is a seven-stage group crisis intervention technique. It is a formal, structured group meeting emphasizing discussion of the facts surrounding the critical incident, ventilation of emotions, normalization of reactions, and stress management education.
- Families and significant others of emergency services workers are a group of very important people that are affected by the tragedy of critical incidents and the stress of daily emergency services work.
- CISM teams and organizations provide referrals and follow-up after a traumatic event.

7

CISD: A Critical Analysis

OBJECTIVES

- Define anecdotal sources.
- Recognize how common sense, belief systems, and relying on authority are not appropriate for scientific research or analysis.
- Describe the scientific method.
- List the key elements of scientific research or journal articles.
- Recognize the limitations of generalizing results of meta-analyses research to CISD and emergency services providers.
- Identify the sample and randomization problems in CISD and emergency services providers research.
- Describe the limitations of outcome measurements in current CISD and emergency services provider research.
- Recognize that personality factors may influence the reactions of emergency services providers to critical incidents and be an area of future research.
- List the four recommendations for improving research of CISD and emergency services providers.

CISM, and particularly CISD, have become an emerging standard of care in crisis intervention and emergency mental health for emergency services providers. Its extensive use is widely cited in the literature. CISD is at the heart of a loose network of hundreds of CISM teams in the United States, Canada, Australia, and Western Europe. Emergency care providers have come to expect CISM services, particularly CISD, after major traumatic events. Recently, the trade magazine, *Journal of Emergency Medical Services* (JEMS), reported that some of New York City's EMS providers were critical of a lack of CISM services following the traumatic events of September 11, 2001 (Dionne, 2002). This criticism came despite many other professional mental health services offered them, including elements of CISM. There have also been a number of informal discussions and arguments among emergency services providers and mental health care professionals regarding the need for and efficacy of CISD. An intervention that is asserted as a standard of care, that is internationally marketed and employed, and that has come to be expected by those whom it serves should be critically analyzed. In the pages that follow, we look at what the researchers are saying about this intervention and how they are arriving at their conclusions. First, reviewing the professional standards of research and why they exist establishes the groundwork for such a critical analysis.

RESEARCH AND THE SCIENTIFIC METHOD

Humans have been analyzing, explaining, and predicting behavior and events for all of recorded history. We do this so that we may understand ourselves and try to improve our lives. There are all kinds of ways to explain behavior. For example, we may use common sense, rely on belief systems, or trust someone in authority. In science, these sources are known as **anecdotal sources**. When it comes to analyzing and explaining such things as medicines, new technical procedures, or interventions such as CISD, these methods have proven to be unreliable and oftentimes faulty. We want to be able to predict with a high degree of accuracy what will happen if we provide some new medicine or intervention to someone. The test is, "Will the concept work?" **Common sense** is not based on careful, systematic observations. It merely *seems* to make sense. It's based on biased, incomplete perceptions, and is not verified against other possible explanations. When a boyfriend and girlfriend find themselves suddenly having to live far apart, someone may say to them, "Absence makes the heart grow fonder!" And someone else may say, "Out of sight, out of mind!" Which is accurate? Common sense may not have the most reliable and effective answers to complex problems. **Relying on belief systems** means that an idea is accepted on faith, typically through upbringing or indoctrination into an organization. Beliefs are handed down through families; they come from a trusted person, group, religious writings, and practices; or they evolve through culture. Little or no verifiable evidence is required; beliefs are simply based on faith. Concepts are simply to be accepted because they are supposed to be inspired or self-evident. They oftentimes are unspoken and involve rules that guide a variety of behavior. Closely related to our belief system, **authority** is another way that people explain and predict behavior. Typical sources of authority can be a television show, a magazine article, a radio personality, a religious figure, or simply because "the doctor said so." Although an authority figure can be a useful place to start an inquiry, authority figures do not always provide valid and reliable answers, either. The source of authority may not truly be authoritative. They could be biased by a particular point of view or they could stand to gain some profit or reward from convincing you about their position. Do you trust your car salesman for information, or do you read what *Consumer Reports* has to say? The car salesman has something personal to gain from what he has to tell you. The same may be true of interventions such as CISM and CISD. That is why psychology uses empiricism and the scientific method to inquire about the nature of problems and what works and what does not work to help solve them (Bordens & Abbott, 1999; Bronowski, 1972; Comer, 1998; Kazdin, 1995; Smock, 1999; Weiten & Lloyd, 2003).

The scientific method has developed in order to avoid the pitfalls of the other ways of analyzing, explaining, and predicting behavior and events. The **scientific method** is made up of four cyclical steps: (1) observing a phenomenon, (2) forming tentative explanations of cause and effect, (3) further observing or experimenting (or both) to rule out alternative explanations, and (4) refining and retesting the explanations (Bordens & Abbott, 1999). The process involves a cyclical rotation between the study process and publication. Results of a scientific study are published in reputable journals for scrutiny by the scientific community. If you are in law enforcement, the science of criminal justice drives part of your line of work. If you are a firefighter, the fire sciences drive part of yours. If you are an emergency medical technician (EMT) or paramedic, the sciences of medicine and emergency prehospital care drive part of your occupation.

This process has unfolded over hundreds of years of philosophical and scientific efforts and has advanced to established methods of inquiry with a unique blend of characteristics. Although a full discussion of these characteristics would be too cumbersome here, the rigorous ideas of empiricism and scientific research are the established standards for analyzing, explaining, and predicting the outcomes of things like emergency services providers and CISD. Before examining what researchers have reported about CISD, there are a few key elements concerning formally reported scientific findings that should be considered.

Key Elements of Reported Research

When critically analyzing scientific research, there are key elements that should be evaluated (Kazdin, 1995). The first element to examine is the **purpose** of the study. The purpose includes the background and context for the study. It reports the current theories and research that make the study useful, important, or of interest. The hypothesis, predictions, or purpose of a study should be clearly stated.

Appraising the **sample** or participants is another element of research analysis. The number of participants in a sample is crucial in statistical analysis. Also, how the sample was obtained and why they were chosen is important. The most reliable sample is one that represents the greater population being studied and is not simply convenient. Demographics, inclusion and exclusion criteria, and informed consent are considered standard items relating to the sample in scientific study.

The **study design** or **method** is crucial in any scientific study. Scientific research is divided into two basic designs: experimental design and correlational design. An experimental design is the classical design that uses an independent variable and a dependent variable. The **independent variable** is a drug or treatment that is manipulated. The **dependent variable** is what is measured or the effect. For example, when studying high blood pressure, the independent variable is a new drug and the dependent variable is the blood pressure. When other variables are controlled, experimental designs discover cause-and-effect relationships. Did the study drug lower blood pressure?

Correlational studies do not demonstrate a cause-and-effect relationship. Correlational studies simply observe the changes in one variable that are associated with the changes in another variable. There are often so many other variables affecting the two tested variables, teasing out any cause and effect between the tested variables becomes statistically difficult, though not entirely impossible. It is generally accepted that causation cannot be inferred from correlational study designs. Whichever design is used, reducing error or contamination of the data is critical. One of the principal ways of reducing error is the random assignment of participants to groups or conditions. Researchers also reduce error by assuring anonymity or confidentiality and eliminating their own personal biases. The idea is to make the research as unbiased and objective as possible.

Key Elements of Scientific Research

- Purpose of the study or hypothesis
- Sample
- Study design or methods
- Outcome measures
- Procedures
- Results
- Discussion

Evaluating the outcome measures is another step in analyzing research. **Outcome measures** are the assessment tools used to measure the changes in the dependent variable or the relationship between the variables. Examples of outcome measurements are personality tests, self-report measures, changes in behavior, or biological measures such as the measurement of a hormone level or pulse rate. The outcome measures chosen should be appropriate, accepted by other researchers, and relate well to the hypothesis and accepted or new theories. The validity and reliability of the measure(s) used is important. The best research uses inventories and scales that have statistically accepted reliability and validity data available and are readily available to other researchers. This allows for replication and future meta-analyses.

The **procedures** implementing the study are then considered. The setting, timing, and potential sources of bias are scrutinized to ensure the study meets rigorous scientific methods.

Finally, the **results** and **discussion** are examined. The statistical analysis of the data collected should follow accepted methods, meet statistical significance, and address the hypothesis and purpose of the study. The major findings of the study and how these add to the body of research and theories should be reported. Limitations of the study and ideas for further research should be reported.

Armed with the knowledge of the key elements of research studies, we can better analyze the studies and the data concerning CISD.

RESEARCH AND CISD

First, some manuals, books, and training courses rely heavily on speculation, theory, and anecdotal sources. Some do not even include bibliographies. Those that do, refer to magazine articles, newspaper articles, and unpublished writings. This is simply garnish for an informal discussion. It may sound good, but there is not much substance. Informed and professional consumers will recognize these for what they are—marketing. These may serve as fine starting points for formal discussions, but they are not research and will not answer the difficult questions facing professionals about emergency services providers and CISD. Those types of sources are not considered research and are not considered here. Unfortunately, traumatic events or critical incidents do not lend themselves to rigorous scientific study. The unpredictable nature of these events makes it difficult to take baseline measurements. Randomizing emergency services providers to receive or not to receive debriefing raises ethical and logistical issues. Implementing randomization may mean splitting groups apart, which may affect outcome measures. These and other issues surrounding the chaotic circumstances of critical incidents simply make studying

CISD and emergency services providers a daunting task. Researchers have been creative by using opportunity samples, retrospective or historical assessments, or quasi-experimental designs in an attempt to overcome these obstacles. Those who have stepped into this quagmire and attempted to answer difficult questions should be applauded.

Search results for published journal articles involving CISD and emergency services providers yields many articles. However, when descriptive reports, review articles, theoretical writings that are not actual scientific studies, and other reports on the impact of critical incidents on emergency services personnel are eliminated, a very limited number of studies involving emergency services providers and the efficacy of CISD research remain. That means that after twenty years of CISM, this author was only able to find 6 studies directly investigating the efficacy of CISD and emergency services providers published in reputable journals (see appendix E). Only one of them met inclusion criteria into a strict meta-analysis, and the intervention in that study deviated from the prescribed Mitchell-model (Carlier, Voerman, & Gersons, 2000). Many authors have echoed Mitchell's call from the mid 1980s for more empirical research (Bisson & Deahl, 1994; Everly et al., 1999; Jenkins, 1996; Raphael & Meldrum, 1995), and a wider range of outcome measures (Deahl, 2000). Unfortunately, that call has not yet been fully answered.

Meta-Analysis Reports

Two meta-analyses of the overall debriefing literature have recently been published, one in *The Lancet* (Van Emmerik, Kamphuis, Hulsbosch, & Emmelkamp, 2002) and the other in *The Cochrane Library* (Rose, Bisson, & Wessely, 2002), both extremely reputable sources. Meta-analyses of research published in respected journals try to answer the big question of the scientific method, "Does the concept work?" The authors of these analyses searched for and gleaned through every published study on the subject they could find. They established inclusion and exclusion criteria that eliminate marginal research, simple descriptive reports, and theoretical reports. Then they applied statistical analyses to the data from those studies that qualify. The authors of the article in *The Lancet* found only 7 articles that could meet their strict inclusion criteria. *The Cochrane Library* meta-analysis of debriefing research could only find 11 articles to include in their analysis. Both articles arrived at similar conclusions: Debriefing is empirically unwarranted and does not necessarily prevent negative effects following traumatic events. In some cases, the authors concluded, debriefing may even be harmful.

The small sampling of studies that could be included in the meta-analyses demonstrates an unfortunate symptom of the difficulty facing researchers of CISD and PD. A meta-analysis by its very definition *should* include strict inclusion and exclusion criteria. However, the studies that met inclusion criteria in the above-mentioned reports were overwhelmingly studies of primary victims and not of emergency services providers. They included such samples as primary burn victims, women who had miscarriages, motor vehicle accident victims, and relatives of seriously ill or injured patients. Only one of the reported studies included in the meta-analysis had a sample of emergency services providers—a group of police officers—and that study did not stringently follow the debriefing models outlined in this text. The question we are left with is, Can the samples, and therefore the data, in those meta-analyses be generalized to secondary victims, especially such a specialized group known as emergency services providers?

In addition to the sampling problem, the types of debriefing processes used with the sample must be examined. In the reports mentioned above, CISD-type (Mitchell-model) interventions and PD (Dyregrov-model) interventions were compared with one-on-one counseling, educational models, and historical group debriefing models. Mitchell and Dyregrov assert that even their two models should not be compared to one another. One has to wonder, then, how these different interventions in the meta-analyses compare. The authors of the meta-analyses even admit that the original researchers did not strictly adhere to the prescribed intervention models. This does not mean that important information cannot be gained from these meta-analyses. One simply has to be skeptical about how much of that information applies to emergency services providers receiving Mitchell-model CISD or Dyregrov-model PD. We cannot ignore what is concluded. But we certainly do not have definitive answers concerning CISD and emergency services providers, either.

Before leaving these meta-analyses, it should be noted that the inclusion criteria and methodology for these meta-analyses were rigorous and exemplary. If criteria for meta-analysis included strict adherence to the debriefing models described in this text and was limited to studies of emergency services providers, there would not have been any data to analyze at all. This means the research on CISD and emergency services workers that *is* reported in the literature does not meet strict standards of the scientific methods described in the first section of this chapter. Two of the biggest problems facing researchers are samples and randomization. Selected reports are critiqued and are representative of the studies investigating emergency services providers and CISD (see appendix E).

The Sample and Randomization Quandary

Jenkins (1996) investigated a sample of emergency services providers exposed to a shocking mass shooting incident in Killeen, Texas, on

October 16, 1991. She found that CISD was correlated with reduced depression and anxiety after one month of exposure. However, it was an emergency services providers' perception of empathy from other people who were not involved with the critical incident that seemed to make the most difference, independent from CISD. So, family, friends, and coworkers *not* involved in the incident that provide empathy and support may be more influential in reducing acute stress symptoms than CISD. The small sample of only 29 EMTs, paramedics, and firefighters is a limitation of this study. This type of sample is known as an opportunity sample; the sample is limited to the opportunistic nature of the critical incident and those who responded who are willing to participate. No inclusion or exclusion criteria are mentioned. There were also methodological limitations. Pre-event perceptions of stress were measured *after* the incident and traditional levels of significance were not used. When authors follow accepted ethical guidelines with an opportunity sample such as this, randomization is not usually possible, either. This is a universal problem in crisis research. Some people choose to attend CISD and participate in research and some do not. Others choose not to participate in CISD or the research. Serious questions about differences between these nonrandomized groups surface. Personality and biological factors, prior traumatic exposure, other stressors, preexisting mental health problems, thoughts and attitudes about CISD, availability of support networks, coworker relationships, and organizational factors are just a few of the variables that could be different between these groups. These differences could be affecting outcomes. Only one of the measures used in this study, the Symptom Check List-90, Revised, was a widely accepted scale with accepted validity and reliability data.

Another study using an opportunity sample investigated the effects of CISD on providers and rescuers following the tragic sinking of a passenger ferry carrying nearly 1,000 passengers and crew (Nurmi, 1999). A group of nurses working in a receiving hospital were compared with the victim identification team, firefighters, and rescuers involved with the incident. The nurses were the only group who did not have CISD. Their scores on three widely accepted measures of traumatization were elevated compared to those who received CISD. Or conversely, those who received CISD had lower traumatization scores. There was one exception. The body identification team had higher scores on one of the three measures, the Impact of Event Scale—Revised. Again, questions about group differences in a nonrandomized sample arise. Are there inherent differences between a group of nurses in an emergency room and a group of firefighters and rescuers on the scene and body handlers who have to identify victims? Are we comparing apples, or are we comparing apples and oranges? One difference immediately apparent was that the air rescuers and firefighters were all male and the nurses were all female. Females are reported in the literature to have a higher rate of PTSD and traumatic symptomatology (Hidalgo & Davidson, 2000). Other variables, such as exposure, education, training, and those mentioned in the previous paragraph that might affect outcomes, are left unknown.

The effects of CISD on police officers involved in shooting incidents were studied over a period of six years in Australia (Leonard & Alison, 1999). Those who participated in a CISD were compared to those who did not. Overall, there were no significant differences in coping behaviors between the groups. There was a trend in the data indicating that those who participated in CISD made greater efforts to remove the stress associated with the event (active coping). In addition, those who participated in CISD tended to make the best of the situation by growing from it or seeing it in a more positive light. They also reported significantly more colleague support compared to the non-CISD group. Whether participating in CISD or not, police officers who had another negative life event sometime in the previous year *and* were involved in a shooting incident, were significantly more vulnerable to maladaptive coping, such as excessive alcohol and drug use. Even though both groups had significantly higher anger levels (state and trait anger scales) than the general population, the non-CISD group had significantly higher anger levels than the CISD group. Similar to other CISD research, the small opportunity sample creates interpretation problems. The authors of this study openly and directly discuss those limitations. First, the analysis demonstrated differences in the severity of incidents between the two groups. The CISD group tended to have more serious incidents than the non-CISD group. Second, those who did not participate in a CISD were either overlooked by police department administration for CISD or simply refused to participate in CISD. It is likely that these two factors combined to create differences that affected outcomes. A recurrent theme of small opportunity samples, nonrandomization, and group differences that could affect outcomes is an apparent limitation of a number of CISD research designs.

Limitations of Outcome Measures

Outcome measures can be another limitation in CISD efficacy research. A reliance on self-report measures is evident in the literature. Selye's and Lazarus's seminal work demonstrated that stress is an interaction between biology and psychology. True to this seminal research, Baum et al. (1982) lay the foundation for measurements in the study of stress. There are four basic types of stress measurements: self-report, performance based, psychophysiological, and biochemical measures. Researchers may choose to rely solely on self-report measures because of limitations of resources, techniques, time, money, and the simplicity of administration. There are problems with this approach, however. Self-report measures tap only one aspect of the process of the stress response. In addition, self-report measures are susceptible to intentional and unintentional biases. Individuals in the midst of a critical incident may not see research questionnaires as a priority issue and may not give the instruments their full attention (Everly et al., 1999). Other problems with self-report measures include symptom reporting bias, social or political concerns, accuracy of self-awareness, and the effect of differing coping styles on self-report measures (Baum et al., 1982). In addition, the dependence on self-report measures and behavioral outcome measures, such as return to work measures, risks the exclusion of biological outcome measures. Baum et al. (1982) advocates a multilevel approach to measuring the multidimensional characteristics of the stress response. When reviewing the literature, none of the reports investigating emergency services workers and CISD or critical incident stress used biochemical outcome measures, and almost all relied solely on self-report measures. In addition to relying on accepted self-report scales, many of the researchers developed their own self-report instruments for which there is little or no reliability and validity data (Bryant & Harvey, 1996; Chemtob, Tomas, Law, & Cremniter, 1997; Harvey-Lintz & Tidwell, 1997; Jenkins, 1996; Marmar, Weiss, Metzler, Ronfeldt, & Foreman, 1996; Nixon et al., 1999; Wee, Mills, & Koehler, 1999). Others used semistructured interviews (Jenkins, 1996; Smith & De Cesnay, 1994; Stuhlmiller, 1994), and some articles had no outcome measures at all and are simply descriptive reports (Budd, 1997; Cigranag, Pace, & Yasuhara, 1995; Everly, 1995; Jiggetts & Hall, 1995; Lane, 1994; Linton, 1995; Walker, 1990).

Studies of Special Mention

One recent study provides some improvement in its sample and outcome measurements (Harris, Baloğlu, & Stacks, 2002). This study used a sample of 660 firefighters from a larger Federal Emergency Management Administration (FEMA) study. Although still an opportunity sample, the sample was large and diverse. The self-report measures used were widely accepted scales with sound validity and reliability data. The authors found no evidence of CISD directly contributing, positively or negatively, either to coping skills or to traumatic stress reactions. They did find a weak link between parameters of personality and CISD, supporting other personality and traumatic exposure research. Even though the sample was very healthy overall, some extreme scores on anxiety, depression, and worldview measures indicate that some personality types may be more vulnerable to critical incidents. Personality measures may be a key source of future research. This led the authors to conclude that organizations may benefit from a change in strategy focus. Intervention models that deal with critical incidents may not be the best approach. Shifting to programs that develop effective pre-employment screening, e.g., adding personality inventories to the screening process, coupled with employee training and preparation, may better serve emergency services organizations and emergency services providers. In contrast to this line of reasoning, however, others have made the argument that the personality traits that make up "hardiness" may not suit the nature of emergency services work (Alexander & Klein, 2001). The area of personality, critical incident stress, CISD, and emergency services providers warrants further research.

The Carlier, Voerman, and Gersons (2000) study included in *The Lancet* meta-analysis investigated 243 police officers exposed to traumatic events. Three successive debriefing sessions that included traumatic stress education were administered at 24 hours, one month, and three months. No significant differences between debriefed, not-debriefed, and controls on measures of psychological distress were found. The high levels of satisfaction with the debriefing process were not correlated with any significant positive outcomes.

Two other studies deserve special mention because of their widespread use in discussions of CISD. As part of a larger study investigating the longitudinal patterns of PTSD, Alexander McFarlane (1988) reported that volunteer firefighters who had delayed PTSD symptoms tended to use the support of colleagues and attend debriefings. He suggests that this support minimizes the stress from the traumatic incident in the short term, but that it does not resolve the trauma resulting in a delayed manifestation of PTSD symptomatology in some firefighters. While this interpretation makes intuitive sense, it was not the focus of this study. No hypotheses or criteria were established for either the assessment of the effects of debriefing or of the debriefing process used. McFarlane states, ". . . their disorder seemed to have grown out of the failure of these attempts to resolve their experience. This failure to 'work through' their traumatic memories may have been due to the influence of other vulnerability factors" (p. 35). Supporting his interpretation is the finding that those who developed acute PTSD symptoms tended to avoid debriefings and shun the support of colleagues.

Another oft-cited study investigated 43 primary victims of Hurricane Iniki (Chemtob et al., 1997). The sample did not include emergency services personnel and did not investigate CISD. It is only cited here because many have referred to this study when discussing CISD. The study compared two small groups. Most of the members of one group were first-time peer counselors of a disaster counseling project for FEMA. The second group was composed of mental health professionals, paraprofessionals, and administrative and clerical staff from a local mental health center. The groups differed significantly in education. Clearly, the second group also had significant mental health work experience. Higher socioeconomic status is correlated with a reduced stress response and increased health (Brunner, 1997) and education level has been shown to mitigate PTSD symptomatology (Begic & Jokic-Begic, 2001; Gold, Engdahl, Eberly, Blake, Page, & Frueh, 2000). The two groups from this small opportunity sample presented with problematic characteristics. The intervention used was not CISD or PD, but rather a psychoeducational model lasting 3 hours followed by 2 hours of lecture on postdisaster recovery. The first group was not debriefed until 6 months after the incident and the second group, 90 days later. Outcome measurements were taken 90 days after the interventions. This time-lagged design, while creative, allows for numerous variables to interplay with such a small sample. Attributing effects to a one-time intervention 9 months and 12 months later in a small opportunity sample without controls or randomization is not sound empiricism. When that information is coupled with the fact that the study is of a small number of primary victims who received an intervention other than CISD, it is problematic to generalize anything from this study to emergency services providers and the efficacy of CISD.

Conclusions on the Efficacy and Use of CISD and PD

Current research on emergency services providers and CISD and PD presents with many problems and limitations. Small opportunity samples, nonrandomization, group differences that could affect outcomes, methodological problems, and the use of nonstandardized outcome measures are all signs of the difficulties facing researchers who want answers to questions about CISD and PD and emergency services workers. The results from these studies are mixed, and it seems that other factors, like personality and others' empathy, may be having more of an influence on the reduction of symptoms and recovery. This does not mean that CISD is not having some positive impact. There just is not conclusive evidence supporting it one way or the other. Changes in research design and implementation are necessary.

First, since opportunity samples may be the most efficient way to gather information about CISD efficacy, larger samples and creative longitudinal designs are necessary. Second, returning to the lab and employing true empirical designs is still an alternative. Third, if data is going to be generalizable, replicable, and available for meta-analysis, researchers need to use standard, widely accepted outcome measures. Finally, outcome measures need to be expanded beyond self-report measures. Other dimensions of the stress response, such as biological and hormonal markers, might tell us more about the reactions of emergency services providers to critical incidents.

The most significant conclusion that one should get from the research is that we still cannot draw any definitive conclusions. Crisis intervention, including CISD, following traumatic or critical incidents is still theoretically and clinically prudent. Until definitive research can paint a clearer picture, it is perhaps legally prudent and the humanly responsible service for organizations to provide. At this point, the rationale of withholding CISD to emergency services providers following a critical incident would not be founded in the research.

Offering other forms of crisis intervention by appropriately trained peer-crisis counselors and/or mental health professionals is also still reasonable and prudent. Reaching out to emergency services workers following critical incidents and offering care, support, and the opportunity to process and connect to others, no matter what the format, is still well-founded in crisis intervention and psychotraumatology theory and practice and in the human spirit. Simply stated however, just what specifically might be harmful or what type of format might be most helpful has not been scientifically established and much work is left to be done.

Key Points

- CISM and CISD should be critically analyzed because it is asserted as a standard of care, is internationally marketed and employed, and has come to be expected by those whom it serves.
- Human beings analyze, explain, and predict behavior and events so that we may understand ourselves and try to improve our lives.
- Anecdotal sources of explanation include using common sense, reliance on belief systems, or trusting someone in authority.
- The scientific method has developed in order to avoid the pitfalls of the other ways of analyzing, explaining, and predicting behavior and events.
- When critically analyzing scientific research, there are key elements that should be evaluated: the purpose, sample, methods, outcome measures, procedures, results, and discussion.
- Although authors of meta-analyses conclude that debriefing is empirically unwarranted, does not necessarily prevent negative effects following traumatic events, and in some cases may even be harmful, problems exist with samples and methodology.
- Two of the biggest problems facing researchers of CISD and emergency services providers are sample problems and randomization.
- Outcome measures can be another limitation in CISD efficacy research, with multidimensional approaches offering the most empirically sound designs.
- Suggestions for improving the research of CISD and emergency services providers include using larger samples, longitudinal designs, employing true empirical designs, using standard, widely accepted outcome measures, and using outcome measures beyond self-report measures.

Glossary

acute stress The sudden and typically short-term stress response usually associated with one specific stressor.

alcohol A legalized and highly addictive central nervous system depressant and toxic chemical associated with many social problems, substance abuse problems, and many psychological and physical disorders.

anecdotal source A source that explains phenomena and that is unreliable and often faulty such as common sense, belief systems, and authority; usually unpublished.

caffeine The most widely used stimulant in the world that stimulates the central nervous system and can trigger the stress response.

chronic stress The low-level stress response associated with long-term stressor. Easily taken for granted, it can be as destructive as any chronic disease process. AKA: cumulative stress or pile-up effect.

CISD Critical Incident Stress Debriefing. A seven-stage group crisis intervention technique that is a formal, structured group meeting emphasizing discussion of the facts surrounding the critical incident (informational elements), ventilation of emotions, normalization of reactions, and stress management education.

CISM Critical Incident Stress Management. The integrated and comprehensive multicomponent program for the provision of crisis and disaster mental health services.

complex carbohydrates Essential dietary requirements providing high energy and low fat. Examples include rice, pasta, and potatoes.

critical incidents Events that have the potential to overwhelm usual coping mechanisms resulting in severe distress in most individuals. AKA: traumatic event or critical event.

dependent variable That which is measured (the effect) in a scientific study; also known as an *outcome measure*.

defusing A flexible, small group discussion of a critical incident usually conducted within 12 hours of the event.

demobilization A group intervention used behind the lines at large-scale incidents to facilitate emergency services workers' transition away from the scene.

diaphragmatic breathing A deep, abdominal form of breathing known to induce the relaxation response.

emergency services workers Those employed or who volunteer in the emergency services profession and their support staff; e.g., firefighters, EMTs, paramedics, law enforcement personnel, dispatchers, hazardous materials specialists.

environmental stressors Aspects of a particular environment that can elicit the stress response. In emergency services this could include things such as noises at the scene, weather, hazardous materials, crowds, and traffic.

fats Essential dietary requirements that contain twice as much energy as carbohydrates. They are designed for prolonged, intense activity, and automatically increases during times of stress. Fats are associated with cardiac disease, stroke, and vessel disease.

fight-or-flight response The complex physiological response to stress involving the sympathetic nervous system and the endocrine system.

holistic approach A healing discipline that incorporates healing and managing stress from a total system approach: mind, body, heart, and spirit.

homeostasis The normal, balanced and yet dynamic state of the body.

immediate interventions Stress management techniques that are readily available following a crisis or stressful event utilized to reduce stress or the stress response.

independent variable The drug or treatment that is manipulated and under investigation in a scientific study.

internal motivation Being less motivated by external factors, such as money, and more motivated by internal factors, such as job satisfaction and values.

long-term interventions Stress management techniques that require learning and developing new skills or participating in therapy in order to reduce stress or the stress response.

major incident An event for which the available resources are insufficient to manage the number of casualties or the nature of the emergency.

massage therapy An age-old stress reduction technique of using physical touch and massage associated with decreasing the stress response and inducing the relaxation response.

meditative prayer An age-old, self-reflective prayer endorsed by every major religion and known to induce the relaxation response and promote a feeling of general well-being and inner peace.

methylated xanthine The active chemical in caffeinated products that can stimulate the fight-or-flight response.

music listening practice The use of music to bring about helpful changes in emotional and/or physical health.

one-on-one Individual acute crisis counseling is usually provided on-scene by trained peers or mental health CISM team members.

premorbid Existing prior to the onset of the current symptoms or illness.

prevalence The number of cases of a particular phenomenon (usually a disease or diagnosis) within a certain time frame; oftentimes lifetime or yearly prevalence rates are reported.

rescue personality The name given to a set of personality traits identified to be predominant in emergency services workers.

scientific method An empirical method developed to analyze, explain, and predict phenomena.

simple sugars Sugars that have been stripped of their nutritional value during processing; found in candy, table sugar, honey, and sodas.

social support system The network of friends and relatives who provide advice, assistance, and someone to confide in.

stress A state of arousal, either pleasant or unpleasant, that places a demand on a person to adapt. A four-part physiological, emotional, and cognitive process that consists of a stressor, the perception of being threatened, a response, and a fourth stage of relaxation or exhaustion.

stress response The physical, cognitive, and emotional changes brought about by the perception of being threatened by a stressor; stress.

stressor A physical, emotional, or cognitive event that elicits the stress response.

traits Relatively enduring and consistent ways of thinking, acting, and feeling that are believed to be the basic units of personality.

unrealistic optimism The dichotomy exemplified by emergency services workers rating their job as more stressful compared with other occupations but also reporting their chances of being adversely affected or harmed by this stress as less than average.

water An essential element required for life and all biological processes. Adequate intake of water is particularly important during stressful periods.

Posttest

1. Emergency services providers includes
   (a) firefighters
   (b) law enforcement
   (c) EMS personnel
   (d) dispatchers
   (e) all of the above

2. A state of arousal, either pleasant or unpleasant, that places a demand on a person to adapt is
   (a) stress
   (b) fight-or-flight
   (c) debriefing
   (d) displacement

3. Sudden stress that is typically more intense and subsides quickly is called
   (a) chronic stress
   (b) general adaptation syndrome
   (c) acute stress
   (d) none of the above

4. The type of stress associated with disease because the body is in a state of arousal for long periods is called
   (a) chronic stress
   (b) general adaptation syndrome
   (c) acute stress
   (d) none of the above

5. The four stages of stress include all of the following EXCEPT
   (a) stressor
   (b) threat perception
   (c) the stress response
   (d) the general adaptation syndrome
   (e) relaxation or exhaustion

6. The stress response starts with an environmental or psychological event called a
   (a) stress response
   (b) stressor
   (c) threat perception
   (d) trauma

7. The complex physiological response to stress is also known in medicine as the
   (a) fight-or-flight response
   (b) stimulation response
   (c) stress–stimulus response
   (d) emergency response

8. Disruption in logical thinking, minor problems seeming unmanageable, and criticism taken more harshly are all examples of
   (a) physiological reactions
   (b) cognitive reactions
   (c) emotional reactions
   (d) behavioral reactions

9. The dichotomy exemplified by emergency services workers rating their job as more stressful compared with other occupations but also reporting their chances of being adversely affected or harmed by this stress as less than average is known as
   (a) cognitive displacement
   (b) unrealistic optimism
   (c) fight-or-flight response
   (d) stress-induced cognitions

10. Sirens, cries for help, moans of pain, angry or threatening voices, radios, and engines are examples of
    (a) personality stressors
    (b) environmental stressors
    (c) affective stressors
    (d) critical incidents

11. Studies reveal that emergency services personnel tend to be internally motivated.
    (a) true
    (b) false

12. Emergency services workers tend to have all of the following personality traits EXCEPT
    (a) need to be in control
    (b) action oriented
    (c) high need for stimulation
    (d) low dedication

13. All of the following are healthy diet items EXCEPT
    (a) complex carbohydrates
    (b) fruits
    (c) vegetables
    (d) water
    (e) fats

14. Sugar, caffeine, and alcohol are encouraged during stressful periods.
    (a) true
    (b) false

15. One of the best ways to return the body to homeostasis is to
    (a) drink alcohol
    (b) avoid contact with others
    (c) communicate
    (d) eat fatty foods

16. Holding in thoughts and feelings and being isolated has been associated with
    (a) longevity
    (b) an increased risk of death
    (c) a healthy lifestyle
    (d) emergency services administrators

17. Diaphragmatic breathing, music therapy, and massage therapy are examples of
    (a) communication techniques
    (b) cognitive therapy
    (c) CISDs debriefings
    (d) relaxation techniques

18. What has a calming effect on the mind's basic thought processes and reduces stress?
    (a) meditative prayer
    (b) critical incidents
    (c) emergency services work
    (d) a diet high in cholesterol

19. Cognitive restructuring, behavior modification, journal writing, art therapy, and communication skills training are all examples of
    (a) short-term interventions
    (b) long-term interventions
    (c) the debriefing process
    (d) none of the above

20. Nausea, anxiety, confusion, and withdrawal are expected reactions to critical incidents.
    (a) true
    (b) false

21. What has such a severe emotional and physical impact that it has the potential to overwhelm usual coping mechanisms resulting in severe distress and impairment in the ability to cope?
    (a) crucial incidents
    (b) composite incidents
    (c) critical incidents
    (d) demobilizations

22. All of the following are associated with high emotional impact on emergency services workers EXCEPT
    (a) knowing or identifying with the victims or with their family
    (b) large-scale incidents
    (c) surprise or novelty of the incident
    (d) loud and noisy incidents

23. One of the most serious potential consequences of critical incidents is
    (a) euphoria
    (b) increased communication
    (c) increased job fulfillment
    (d) PTSD

24. An integrated and comprehensive multicomponent program for the provision of crisis and disaster mental health services is
    (a) CISM
    (b) CISD
    (c) general adaptation syndrome
    (d) cognitive therapy

25. Individual acute crisis counseling that is usually provided on-scene by trained peers or mental health CISM team members is known as a
    (a) CISD
    (b) demobilization
    (c) defusing
    (d) one-on-one

26. The most popular element of the CISM program that is utilized by emergency services personnel after a critical incident is a
    (a) CISD
    (b) demobilization
    (c) defusing
    (d) one-on-one

27. A formal, structured group meeting that emphasizes discussion of the facts surrounding a critical incident, ventilation of emotions, normalization of reactions, and stress management education is known as a
    (a) CISD
    (b) demobilization
    (c) defusing
    (d) one-on-one

28. A debriefing model that places emphasis on the group leader and process is known as
    (a) CISD
    (b) CISM
    (c) PD
    (d) PISD

29. All of the following are rules used during a CISD EXCEPT
    (a) strict confidentiality
    (b) no recordings, taping, or notes
    (c) multiple breaks will be taken
    (d) no food, drinks, or tobacco products

30. Families are people who are affected by the tragedy of critical incidents and are often forgotten.
    (a) true
    (b) false

31. Emergency services providers are considered _____ victims after a critical incident.
    (a) primary
    (b) secondary
    (c) tertiary
    (d) binary

32. Family members and significant others are considered _____ victims after a critical incident.
    (a) primary
    (b) secondary
    (c) tertiary
    (d) binary

33. Abuse or violence toward a family member or significant other by an EMS provider after a critical incident is considered:
    (a) direct impact
    (b) indirect impact
    (c) secondary impact
    (d) critical incident impact

34. When an emergency services provider isolates him- or herself from family or significant others after a critical incident, it is known as
    (a) direct impact
    (b) indirect impact
    (c) secondary impact
    (d) critical incident impact

35. Reasons for referring an emergency services provider after a critical incident include all of the following EXCEPT
    (a) administrative reprimands
    (b) mental health services
    (c) medical services
    (d) legal services

36. A source that explains phenomena and that is unreliable and often faulty such as common sense, belief systems, and authority and is usually unpublished is called
    (a) scientific
    (b) empirical
    (c) independently unreliable
    (d) anecdotal

37. An empirical method developed to analyze, explain, and predict phenomena is known as the
    (a) scientific method
    (b) empirical process
    (c) study method
    (d) anecdotal method

38. All of the following are key elements of reported research EXCEPT
    (a) purpose of the study
    (b) sample
    (c) study design
    (d) scientific critique

39. Which of the following statements about the efficacy of CISD and emergency services providers is true?
    (a) An abundance of efficacy studies have been published.
    (b) Results from these studies clearly demonstrate the efficacy of CISD.
    (c) Results from these studies clearly demonstrate that CISD does not work.
    (d) Results from these studies are mixed and problematic.

40. Current research on CISD and emergency services providers present with many problems and limitations.
    (a) true
    (b) false

Answers to Posttest

1. e	21. c
2. a	22. d
3. d	23. d
4. a	24. a
5. d	25. d
6. b	26. a
7. a	27. a
8. b	28. a
9. b	29. c
10. b	30. a
11. a	31. b
12. d	32. c
13. e	33. a
14. b	34. b
15. c	35. a
16. b	36. d
17. d	37. a
18. a	38. d
19. b	39. d
20. a	40. a

APPENDIX A

DSM-IV Diagnostic Criteria for Acute Stress Disorder (ASD)

A. Exposure to a traumatic event that involves both:
   1. Witnessing or confronting an event(s) that involved actual or threatened death or serious injury, or threat to the physical integrity of self or others; and,
   2. Response involved intense fear, helplessness, or horror.

B. During or after the experience of the distressing event, the individual has three or more of the following dissociative symptoms:
   1. Subjective sense of numbing, detachment, or absence of emotional responsiveness.
   2. A reduction in awareness of his or her surroundings (e.g., "being in a daze").
   3. Derealization.
   4. Depersonalization.
   5. Dissociative amnesia (i.e., inability to recall an important aspect of the trauma).

C. The traumatic event is persistently reexperienced in at least one of the following ways:
   1. Recurrent and intrusive distressing recollections of the event, including images, thoughts, or perceptions.
   2. Recurrent distressing dreams of the event.
   3. Acting or feeling as if the traumatic event were recurring (includes a sense of reliving the experience, illusions, hallucinations, and dissociative flashback episodes, including those that occur on awakening or when intoxicated).

4. Intense psychological distress at exposure to internal or external cues that symbolize or resemble an aspect of the traumatic event.
5. Physiological reactivity on exposure to internal or external cues that symbolize or resemble an aspect of the traumatic event.

D. Marked avoidance of stimuli that arouse recollections of the trauma (e.g., thoughts, feelings, conversations, activities, places, people).

E. Marked symptoms of anxiety or increased arousal such as:
   1. Difficulty falling asleep or staying asleep.
   2. Irritability or outbursts of anger.
   3. Difficulty concentrating.
   4. Hypervigilance.
   5. Exaggerated startle response.
   6. Motor restlessness.

F. The disturbance causes clinically significant distress or impairment in social, occupational, or other important areas of functioning or impairs the individual's ability to pursue some necessary task, such as obtaining necessary assistance or mobilizing personal resources by telling family members about the traumatic experience.

G. The disturbance lasts for a minimum of 2 days and a maximum of 4 weeks and occurs within 4 weeks of the traumatic event.

H. The disturbance is not due to the direct physiological effects of a substance (e.g., drug abuse, medications) or a general medical condition.

Adapted with permission from the Diagnostic and Statistical Manual of Mental Disorders, *Text Revision, Copyright 2000. American Psychiatric Association.*

DSM-IV Diagnostic Criteria for Posttraumatic Stress Disorder (PTSD)

A. Exposure to a traumatic event that involves both:
   1. Witnessing or confronting an event(s) that involved actual or threatened death or serious injury, or threat to the physical integrity of self or others; and,
   2. Response involved intense fear, helplessness, or horror.

B. Persistent reexperience of the traumatic event in one or more of the following ways:
   1. Recurrent and intrusive distressing recollections of the event, including images, thoughts, or perceptions.
   2. Recurrent distressing dreams of the event.
   3. Acting or feeling as if the traumatic event were recurring (includes a sense of reliving the experience, illusions, hallucinations, and dissociative flashback episodes, including those that occur on awakening or when intoxicated).
   4. Intense psychological distress at exposure to internal or external cues that symbolize or resemble an aspect of the traumatic event.
   5. Physiological reactivity on exposure to internal or external cues that symbolize or resemble an aspect of the traumatic event.

C. Persistent avoidance of stimuli associated with the trauma and numbing of general responsiveness (not present before the trauma), as indicated by 3 or more of the following:
   1. Efforts to avoid thoughts, feelings, or conversation associated with the trauma.
   2. Efforts to avoid activities, places, or people that arouse recollections of the trauma.
   3. Inability to recall an important aspect of the trauma.
   4. Markedly diminished interest or participation in significant activities.
   5. Feeling of detachment or estrangement from others.
   6. Restricted range of affect (e.g., unable to have loving feelings).
   7. Sense of foreshortened future (e.g., does not expect to have a career, marriage, children, or a normal life span).

D. Persistent symptoms of increased arousal (not present before the trauma), as indicated by 2 or more of the following:
   1. Difficulty falling asleep or staying asleep.
   2. Irritability or outbursts of anger.
   3. Difficulty concentrating.
   4. Hypervigilance.
   5. Exaggerated startle response.

E. Duration of the disturbance is more than 1 month.
F. The disturbance causes clinically significant distress or impairment in social, occupational, or other important areas of functioning.

Specify if:
   Acute: if duration of symptoms is less than 3 months.
   Chronic: if duration of symptoms is 3 months or more.

Specify if:
   With Delayed Onset: if onset of symptoms is at least 6 months after the stressor.

Adapted with permission from the Diagnostic and Statistical Manual of Mental Disorders, *Text Revision, Copyright 2000. American Psychiatric Association.*

APPENDIX B

The Formal CISD Process Consists of Seven Stages or Phases

INTRODUCTION PHASE

In the first phase, team members introduce themselves and establish rapport, preview the debriefing process, set expectations, increase motivation, and set the ground rules.

FACT PHASE

This phase allows the participants to describe what their individual roles and job duties were at the event, and what they saw happen from their point of view. This is prompted by the group leader in an orderly fashion. This factual structuring allows a more complete picture of the event to unfold and encourages participation. It usually begins with the leader asking, "Describe what your role was at the scene. What happened from your point of view?"

THOUGHT PHASE

In this third phase, a transition begins that allows participants to gradually shift from a fact-oriented process to a thought-oriented process. Cognitive reactions are solicited, and transition to the affective domain often begins. A prompting question might be, "What were your first thoughts in response to this event?" or "When did you realize this was going to be an unusual event?"

REACTION PHASE

During this fourth phase, the most highly charged emotional reactions emerge and cathartic ventilation is allowed. This may be initiated by asking, "What was the worst part of the incident for you personally?"

SYMPTOM PHASE

Recognizing and verbalizing physical and psychological symptoms or reactions to the event allows for a transition from the affective domain back to the cognitive domain. The group leader guides this return while understanding that stabilization is a primary goal.

TEACHING PHASE

After identifying some symptoms, a move up the cognitive continuum continues. Normalizing and demedicalizing the crisis reactions and teaching basic personal stress management and coping techniques are accomplished.

REENTRY PHASE

The seventh and final phase offers a last opportunity to reinforce constructive coping mechanisms, identify dysfunctional ones, answer any final questions, and provide for psychological closure to the crisis event. Assessment for the need for follow-up or referrals may also take place.

Adapted from Everly (1995) and Everly and Mitchell (1999).

APPENDIX C

CISM: The Seven Core Elements

	Intervention	Timing	Activation	Goals	Format
1.	Precrisis preparation	Precrisis phase	Anticipation of crisis	Set expectations, improve coping, education	Groups Organizations
2.	Demobilizations	Shift disengagement or immediately postcrisis Usually at large events	Event driven	To inform, and consult To allow for psychological decompression Stress management	Large groups Organizations
3.	Individual crisis counseling	Anytime	Symptom driven	Symptom mitigation Return to function Referral, if needed Stress management	Individuals
4.	Defusings	Postcrisis (within 12 hours)	Usually symptom driven	Symptom mitigation Possible closure Triage	Small groups
5.	CISD	Postcrisis (1–10 days); 3–4 weeks for mass disasters	Usually symptom driven Can be event driven	Facilitate psychological closure Symptom mitigation Triage and possible referral	Small groups
6.	Family crisis intervention	Anytime	Symptom or event driven	Foster support, communications Symptom mitigation Closure, if possible Referral, if needed	Families Organizations
7.	Follow-up and referral	Anytime	Usually symptom driven	Assess mental status Access higher level of care	Individual Family

Adapted from Everly and Mitchell (1999).

APPENDIX D

International Critical Incident Stress Foundation, Inc.
10176 Baltimore National Pike, Unit 201
Ellicott City, MD 21042
Telephone: (410) 750-9600
Fax: (410) 750-9601
(410) 313-2473 (Emergency)
http://www.icisf.org

APPENDIX E

Listing of published journal articles that involved a study specifically designed to relate to the efficacy of CISD and emergency services providers found in a search of Academic Search Premiere, EBSCO Publishing's Psychological and Behavioral Sciences Collection, Medline, PsychINFO, and a manual search of reference lists of articles and selected books.

Carlier, I. V., Voerman, A. E., & Gersons, B. P. (2000). The influence of occupational debriefing on post-traumatic stress symptomatology in traumatized police officers. *British Journal of Medical Psychology, 73*(Pt. 1), 87–98.

Harris, M. B., Baloğlu, M., & Stacks, J. R. (2002). Mental health of trauma-exposed firefighters and critical incident stress debriefing. *Journal of Loss and Trauma, 7*, 223–238.

Jenkins, S. R. (1996). Social support and debriefing efficacy among emergency medical workers after a mass shooting incident. *Journal of Social Behavior and Personality, 11*(3), 477–492.

Leonard, R., & Alison, L. (1999). Critical incident stress debriefing and its effects on coping strategies and anger in a sample of Australian police officers involved in shooting incidents. *Work & Stress, 13*(2), 144–161.

Nurmi, L. A. (1999). The sinking of the Estonia: The effects of critical incident stress debriefing (CISD) on rescuers. *International Journal of Emergency Mental Health, 1*, 23–31.

Wee, D. F., Mills, D. M., & Koehler, G. (1999). The effects of critical incident stress debriefing (CISD) on emergency services personnel following the Los Angeles civil disturbance. *International Journal of Emergency Mental Health, 1*, 33–37.

Listing of published journal articles that involved a meta-analysis of debriefings with a variety of samples and debriefing processes found in a search of Academic Search Premiere, EBSCO Publishing's Psychological and Behavioral Sciences Collection, Medline, PsychINFO, and a manual search of reference lists of articles and selected books.

Rose, S., & Bisson, J. (1998). Brief early psychological interventions following trauma: A systematic review of the literature. *Journal of Traumatic Stress,* 11(4), 697–710.

Rose, S., Bisson, J., & Wessely, S. (2002). Psychological debriefing for preventing post traumatic stress disorder (PTSD) (Cochrane Review). In *The Cochrane Library* (vol. 4). Oxford: Update Software.

Van Emmerik, A. A. P., Kamphuis, J. H., Hulsbosch, A. M., & Emmelkamp, P. M. G. (2002). Single session debriefing after psychological trauma: A meta-analysis. *The Lancet, 360,* 766–771.

Bibliography

Alexander, D. A., & Klein, S. (2001). Ambulance personnel and critical incidents. *British Journal of Psychiatry, 178,* 76–81.

About AMTA. (2000). Retrieved October 31, 2003, available from http://www.amtamassage.org.

American Psychiatric Association. (1980). *Diagnostic and statistical manual of mental disorders* (3rd ed.). Washington, DC: Author.

American Psychiatric Association. (1987). *Diagnostic and statistical manual of mental disorders* (3rd ed., Revised). Washington, DC: Author.

American Psychiatric Association. (1994). *Diagnostic and statistical manual of mental disorders* (4th ed.). Washington, DC: Author.

Anshel, M. H. (2000). A conceptual model and implications for coping with stressful events in police work. *Criminal Justice and Behavior, 27,* 375–400.

Baldwin, J. D., & Baldwin, J. I. (1998). *Behavior principles in everyday life* (3rd ed.). Upper Saddle River, NJ: Prentice Hall.

Barlow, D., & Durand, V. M. (1999). *Abnormal psychology* (2nd ed.). Pacific Grove, CA: Brooks/Cole.

Baum, A., Grunberg, N. E., & Singer, J. E. (1982). The use of neuroendocrinological measurements in the study of stress. *Health Psychology, 1,* 217–236.

Beaton, R. D., & Murphy, S. A. (1993). Sources of occupational stress among firefighter/EMTs and firefighter/paramedics and correlations with job-related outcomes. *Prehospital and Disaster Medicine, 8,* 140–150.

Begic, D., & Jokic-Begic, N. (2001). Aggressive behavior in combat veterans with post-traumatic stress disorder. *Military Medicine, 166,* 671–676.

Bisson, J. I. (1997). Is post-traumatic stress disorder preventable? *Journal of Mental Health, 6,* 109–111.

Bisson, J. I., & Deahl, M. P. (1994). Psychological debriefing and prevention of post-traumatic stress: More research is needed. *British Journal of Psychiatry, 165,* 717–720.

Bordens, K. S., & Abbott, B. B. (1999). *Research designs and methods: A process approach* (4th ed.). Mountainview, CA: Mayfield Publishing Company.

Boudreaux, E., Jones, G. N., Mandry, C., & Brantley, P. J. (1996). Patient care and daily stress among emergency medical technicians. *Prehospital and Disaster Medicine, 11*(3), 188–193.

Bramsen, I., & Dirkzwager, A. J. E. (2000). Predeployment personality traits and exposure to trauma as predictors of posttraumatic stress symptoms: A prospective study of former peacekeepers. *American Journal of Psychiatry, 157,* 1115–1120.

Bronowski, J. (1972). *Science and human values* (rev. ed.). New York: Harper & Row.

Brunner, E. (1997). Socioeconomic determinants of health: Stress and the biology of inequality. *British Journal of Medicine, 314,* 1472–1476.

Bryant, R. A., & Harvey, A. G. (1995). Posttraumatic stress in volunteer firefighters: Predictors of distress. *Journal of Nervous and Mental Disease, 183,* 267–271.

Bryant, R. A., & Harvey, A. G. (1996). Posttraumatic stress reactions in volunteer firefighters. *Journal of Traumatic Stress, 9,* 51–62.

Budd, F. (1997). Helping the helpers after the bombing in Dhahran: Critical incident stress services for an air rescue squadron. *Military Medicine, 162,* 515–520.

Carlier, I. V., Voerman, A. E., & Gersons, B. P. (2000). The influence of occupational debriefing on post-traumatic stress symptomatology in traumatized police officers. *British Journal of Medical Psychology, 73*(Pt. 1), 87–98.

Chemtob, C. M., Tomas, S., Law, W., & Cremniter, D. (1997). Postdisaster psychosocial intervention: A field study of the impact of debriefing on psychological distress. *American Journal of Psychiatry, 154,* 415–417.

Cigranag, J., Pace, J., & Yasuhara, T. (1995). Critical incident stress intervention following fatal air mishaps. *Aviation, Space, and Environmental Medicine, 66,* 880–882.

Costa, P. T., & McCrae, R. R. (1997). Stability and change in personality assessment: The revised NEO Personality Inventory in the year 2000. *Journal of Personality Assessment, 68,* 86–94.

Comer, R. J. (1998). *Abnormal psychology* (3rd ed.). New York: W. H. Freeman and Company.

De Mello, A. (1992). *Awareness: The perils and opportunities of reality.* New York: Doubleday.

Deahl, M. P., Srinivasan, M., Jones, N., Neblett, C., & Jolly, A. (2001). Evaluating psychological debriefings: Are we measuring the right outcomes? *Journal of Traumatic Stress, 14,* 527–529.

Dionne, L. (2002, September). After the fall. *Journal of Emergency Medical Services,* 36–57.

Dyregrov, A. (1997). The process in psychological debriefings. *Journal of Traumatic Stress, 10,* 589–605.

Dyregrov, A. (1999). Helpful and hurtful aspects of psychological debriefing groups. *International Journal of Emergency Mental Health, 3,* 175–181.

Everly, G. S. (1995). The role of critical incident stress debriefing (CISD) process in disaster counseling. *Journal of Mental Health Counseling, 17,* 278–290.

Everly, G. S. (1996). Psychotraumatology. In G. S. Everly & J. M. Lating (Eds.), *Psychotraumatology.* Baltimore: Chevron.

Everly, G. S., & Mitchell, J. T. (1999). *Critical incident stress management: A new era and standard of care in crisis intervention* (2nd ed.). Baltimore: Chevron.

Everly, G. S., Flannery, R. B., & Mitchell, J. T. (1999). Critical incident stress management (CISM): A review of the literature. *Aggression and Violent Behavior, 5,* 23–40.

Friedman, M. J. (1996). Biological approaches to the diagnosis and treatment of post-traumatic stress disorder. In G. S. Everly & J. M. Lating, (Eds.), *Psychotraumatology.* Baltimore: Chevron.

Garbarino, S., Beelke, M., Costa, G., Violani, C., Lucidi, F., Ferrillo, F., & Sannita, W. G. (2002). Brain function and effects of shift work: Implications for clinical neuropharmacology. *Neuropsychobiology, 45,* 50–56.

Garbarino, S., De Carli, F., Nobili, L., Mascialino, B., Squarcia, S., Penco, M. A., Beelke, M., Ferrila, F. (2002). Sleepiness and sleep disorders in shift workers: A study on a group of Italian police officers. *Sleep, 25,* 648–653.

Greenstone, J. L. (1993). *Critical incident stress debriefing and crisis management* [Brochure]. Fort Worth, TX: Author and The Texas Department of Health, Bureau of Emergency Management.

Gold, P. B., Engdahl, B. E., Eberly, R. E., Blake, R. J., Page, W. F., & Frueh, B. C. (2000). Trauma exposure, resilience, social support, and PTSD construct validity among former prisoners of war. *Social Psychiatry & Psychiatric Epidemiology, 35,* 36–43.

Harris, M. B., Baloğlu, M., & Stacks, J. R. (2002). Mental health of trauma-exposed firefighters and critical incident stress debriefing. *Journal of Loss and Trauma, 7,* 223–238.

Harvey-Lintz, T., & Tidwell, R. (1997). Effects of the 1992 Los Angeles civil unrest: Post traumatic stress disorder symptomatology among law enforcement officers. *Social Science Journal, 34,* 171–184.

Hidalgo, R. B., & Davidson, J. R. (2000). Posttraumatic stress disorder: Epidemiology and health-related considerations. *Journal of Clinical Psychiatry, Special Issue: New Strategies for the Treatment of Posttraumatic Stress Disorder, 61,* 5–13.

Janik, J. (1992). Addressing cognitive defenses in critical incident stress. *Journal of Traumatic Stress, 5,* 497–503.

Jenkins, S. R. (1996). Social support and debriefing efficacy among emergency medical workers after a mass shooting incident. *Journal of Social Behavior and Personality, 11,* 477–492.

Jiggetts, S. M., & Hall, J. P. (1995). Helping the helper: 528th combat stress center in Somalia. *Military Medicine, 160,* 275–277.

Karlsson, B., Knutsson, A., & Lindahl, B. (2001). Is there an association between shift work and having a metabolic syndrome? Results from a population based study of 27,485 people. *Occupational and Environmental Medicine, 58,* 747–752.

Kazdin, A. E. (1995). Preparing and evaluating research reports. *Psychological Assessment, 7,* 228–237.

Kitamura, T., Onishi, K., Dohi, K., Okinaka, T., Ito, M., Isaka, N., et al. (2002). Circadian rhythm of blood pressure is transformed from a dipper to a non-dipper pattern in shift workers with hypertension. *Journal of Human Hypertension, 16,* 193–197.

Kornfield, J. (1993). *A path with heart: A guide through the perils and promises of spiritual life.* New York: Bantam Books.

Kowalski, R. E. (1989). *The 8-week cholesterol cure* (Rev. ed.). New York: Harper & Row.

Lane, P. S. (1994). Critical incident stress debriefing for health care workers. *Omega: Journal of Death and Dying, 28,* 301–315.

Lazarus, R. S. (1966). *Psychological stress and the coping process.* New York: McGraw-Hill.

Lazarus, R. S., & Folkman, S. (1984). *Stress, appraisal, and coping.* New York: Springer Publishing Company.

Leonard, R., & Alison, L. (1999). Critical incident stress debriefing and its effects on coping strategies and anger in a sample of Australian police officers involved in shooting incidents. *Work & Stress, 13,* 144–161.

Linton, J. C. (1995). Acute stress management with public safety personnel: Opportunities for clinical training and pro bono community service. *Professional Psychology: Research and Practice, 26,* 566–573.

Maguire, B. J., Hunting, K. L., Smith, G. S., & Levick, N. R. (2002). Occupational fatalities in emergency medical services: A hidden crisis. *Annals of Emergency Medicine, 40,* 625–632.

Marmar, C. R., Weiss, D. S., Metzler, T. J., Ronfeldt, H. M., Foreman, C. (1996). Stress responses of emergency services personnel to the Loma Prieta earthquake Interstate 880 freeway collapse and control traumatic incidents. *Journal of Traumatic Stress, 9,* 63–85.

Marmar, C. R., Weiss, D. S., Metzler, T. J., & Delucchi, K. (1996). Characteristics of emergency services personnel related to peritraumatic dissociation during critical incident exposure. *American Journal of Psychiatry, 153*(7), 94–102.

Marmar, C. R., Weiss, D. S., Metzler, T. J., Delucchi, K., Best, S. R., & Wentworth, K. A. (1999). Longitudinal course and predictors of continuing distress following critical incident exposure in emergency services personnel. *Journal of Nervous and Mental Disease, 187,* 15–22.

Maslach, C., & Jackson, S. E. (1981). The measurement of experienced burnout. *Journal of Occupational Behaviour, 2,* 99–113.

McCrae, R. R., & Costa, P. T. (1997). Personality trait structure as a human universal. *American Psychologist, 52,* 509–617.

McCrae, R. R., & Oliver, J. P. (1992). An introduction to the Five-Factor Model and its applications. *Journal of Personality, 60,* 175–215.

McDermott, J. H. (2000). Antioxidant nutrients: Current dietary recommendations and research update. *Journal of the American Pharmaceutical Association, 40*(6), 785–799.

McFarlane, A. C. (1988). The longitudinal course of posttraumatic morbidity: The range of outcomes and their predictors. *Journal of Nervous and Mental Disease, 176,* 30–39.

McFarlane, A. C. (1997). The prevalence and longitudinal course of PTSD: Implications for the neurobiological models of PTSD. *Annals of the New York Academy of Sciences, 821,* 10–23.

Mitchell, J. T. (1983). When disaster strikes…the critical incident stress debriefing process. *Journal of Emergency Services, 8,* 36–39.

Mitchell, J. T., & Bray, G. (1994). *Emergency services stress: Guidelines for preserving the health and careers of emergency services personnel.* Upper Saddle River, NJ: Prentice Hall.

Moran, C. C., & Colless, E. (1995). Perceptions of work stress in Australian firefighters. *Work & Stress, 9,* 405–415.

Neely, K. W., & Spitzer, W. J. (1997). A model for a statewide critical incident stress (CIS) debriefing program for emergency services personnel. *Prehospital and Disaster Medicine, 12,* 114–119.

Nixon, S. J., Schorr, J., Boudreaux, A., & Vincent, R. D. (1999). Perceived sources of support and their effectiveness for Oklahoma City firefighters. *Psychiatric Annals, 29,* 101–105.

North, C. S., McMillen, J. C., Pfefferbaum, B., Spitznagel, E. L., Cox, J., Nixon, S., Bunch, K. P., & Smith, E. M. (2002). Psychiatric disorders in rescue workers after the Oklahoma City bombing. *American Journal of Psychiatry, 159,* 857–859.

Nurmi, L. A. (1999). The sinking of the Estonia: The effects of critical incident stress debriefing (CISD) on rescuers. *International Journal of Emergency Mental Health, 1,* 23–31.

Ornish, D. (1990). *Dr. Dean Ornish's program for reversing heart disease: The only system scientifically proven to reverse heart disease without drugs or surgery.* New York: Ballatine Books.

Palmer, R. G., & Spaid, W. M. (1996). Authoritarianism, inner/other directedness, and sensation seeking in firefighter/paramedics: Their relationship with burnout. *Prehospital and Disaster Medicine, 11,* 11–15.

Pennebaker, J. W., & Susman, J. R. (1988). Disclosure of traumas and psychosomatic processes. *Social Science and Medicine, 26,* 327–332.

Pennebaker, J. W., Hughes, C. F., & O'Heeron, R. C. (1987). The psychophysiology of confession: Linking inhibitory and psychosomatic processes. *Journal of Personality and Social Psychology, 52,* 781–793.

Piedmont, R. L. (1993). A longitudinal analysis of burnout in the health care setting: The role of personal dispositions. *Journal of Personality Assessment, 61,* 457–473.

Raphael, B., & Meldrum. L. (1995). Does debriefing after psychological trauma work? *British Medical Journal, 310,* 1479–1480.

Regehr, C., Goldberg, G., Glancy, G. D., & Knott, T. (2002). Posttraumatic symptoms and disability in paramedics. *Canadian Journal of Psychiatry, 47,* 953–958.

Robinson, H. M., Sigman, M., & Wilson, J. P. (1997). Duty-related stressors and PTSD symptoms in suburban police officers. *Psychological Reports, 81*(Pt.1), 835–845.

Rose, S., & Bisson, J. (1998). Brief early psychological interventions following trauma: A systematic review of the literature. *Journal of Traumatic Stress, 11,* 697–710.

Rose, S., Bisson, J., & Wessely, S. (2002). Psychological debriefing for preventing post traumatic stress disorder (PTSD) [Cochrane Review]. In *The Cochrane Library,* (vol. 4). Oxford: Update Software.

Saigh, P. A., & Bremner, J. D. (1999). The history of posttraumatic stress disorder. In P.A. Saigh & J. D. Bremner (Eds.), *Posttraumatic stress disorder: A comprehensive text* (pp. 1–17). Needham Heights, MA: Allyn & Bacon.

Salmon, P. (2001). Effects of physical exercise on anxiety, depression, and sensitivity to stress: A unifying theory. *Clinical Psychology Review, 21,* 33–61.

Sanders, M. J. (1994). *Mosby's paramedic textbook.* St. Louis, MO: Mosby Lifeline.

Seaward, B. (1994). *Managing stress.* Boston: Jones and Bartlett.

Selye, H. (1956). *The stress of life.* New York: McGraw-Hill.

Shelton, R., & Kelley, J. (1995). *EMS stress: An emergency responder's handbook for living well.* Carlsbad, CA: JEMS Communications.

Simeons, A. T. W. (1961). *Man's presumptuous brain: An evolutionary interpretation of psychosomatic diseases.* New York: E. P. Dutton.

Smith, C. L., & De Cesnay, M. (1994). Critical incident stress debriefings for crisis management in post-traumatic stress disorders. *Medicine and Law, 13*, 185–191.

Smock, T. K. (1999). *Physiological psychology: A neuroscience approach.* Upper Saddle River, NJ: Prentice Hall.

Steinberg, A., & Ritzmann, R. F. (1990). A living systems approach to understanding the concept of stress. *Behavioral Science, 35*, 138–147.

Stuhlmiller, C. M. (1994). Occupational meanings and coping practices of rescue workers in an earthquake disaster. *Western Journal of Nursing Research, 16*, 268–287.

Thorne, M. B., & Henley, T. B. (1997). *Connections in the history and systems of psychology.* Boston: Houghton Mifflin Company.

Van Emmerik, A. A. P., Kamphuis, J. H., Hulsbosch, A. M., & Emmelkamp, P. M. G. (2002). Single session debriefing after psychological trauma: a meta-analysis. *The Lancet, 360*, 766–771.

Vettor, S. M., & Kosinski, F. A. (2000). Work-stress burnout in emergency medical technicians and the use of early recollections. *Journal of Employment Counseling, 37*, 216–228.

Walker, G. (1990). Crisis-care in critical incident debriefing. *Death Studies, 14*, 121–133.

Wee, D. F., Mills, D. M., & Koehler, G. (1999). The effects of critical incident stress debriefing (CISD) on emergency services personnel following the Los Angeles civil disturbance. *International Journal of Emergency Mental Health, 1*, 33–37.

Weiss, D. S., Marmar, C. R., Metzler, T. J., & Ronfeldt, H. M. (1995). Predicting symptomatic distress in emergency services personnel. *Journal of Consulting and Clinical Psychology, 63*, 361–368.

Weiten, W., & Lloyd, M. A. (2003). *Psychology applied to modern life.* Belmont, CA: Wadsworth/Thomson Learning.

Werner, H. R., Bates, G. W., Bell, R. C., Murdoch, P., & Robinson, R. (1992). Critical incident stress in Victoria state emergency service volunteers: Characteristics of critical incidents, common stress responses, and coping methods. *Australian Psychologist, 27*, 159–165.

Wilson, J. L. (2002). The impact of shift patterns on healthcare professionals. *Journal of Nursing Management, 10*(4), 211–219.

Wilson, J. P. (1996). The historical evolution of PTSD diagnostic criteria: From Freud to DSM-IV. In G. S. Everly & J. M. Lating (Eds.), *Psychotraumatology* (pp. 9–26). Baltimore: Chevron.

Yalom, I. D. (1995). *The theory and practice of group psychotherapy* (4th ed.). New York: Basic Books.

Young, A. (2000). An alternative history of traumatic stress. In A. Y. Shalev, R. Yehuda, and A. C. McFarlane (Eds.), *International handbook of human response to trauma* (pp. 51–66). New York: Kluwer Academic/Plenum Publishers.

Index

A
action oriented, 27
aggression, 9
alcohol, 15
Allen, Roger, 21
ambiguity, 28
anecdotal sources, 61
antioxidants, 14
approach coping, 10
art therapy, 21
authority, 62
avoidance coping, 10

B
behavior modification, 21
  classical conditioning, 21
  Pavlovian conditioning, 21
behaviorism
  founder of, 21
  Skinner, B. F., 21
blood glucose, 15
burnout, 29
  effects of, 30

C
caffeine, 15
Canon, Walter, 5
cardiovascular, 14, 28
catharsis, 10
classical conditioning, 21
clotting factors, 14
cognitive restructuring, 21
common sense, 61
communication, 17
complex carbohydrates, 14
coping
  aggression and, 9
  approach coping, 10
  avoidance coping, 10
  defined, 9
  giving up, 10
  learned helplessness and, 10
coping styles. *See* coping
correlational studies, 63
critical incident stress debriefing (CISD), 53
  as a standard of care, 61
  goals of, 54
  research and, 64
  rules of, 55
critical incident stress management (CISM)
  core elements of, 51
  defined, 51
  follow-ups, 57
  referrals, 57
critical incidents
  common features of, 35
  defined, 32
  examples of, 33
  families affected by, 57
  frequency rate, 34
  reactions to, 37
  term coined by, 32

D
defusing, 53
demobilization, 52
dependent variable, 63
depersonalization, 29
diaphragmatic breathing, 17
diet, 13
direct impact, 57

E
Ellis, Albert, 21
emergency services providers
  defined, 24
  occupational fatality rates, 34
  shift-work, 24, 28
environmental stressors, 25
exercise, 16

F
fats, 13
fight-or-flight, 4, 5, 9, 15, 74, 76
  methylated xanthine, 15
flashbacks, 45
follow-up, 57
Frankl, Victor, 21
Freud, Sigmund, 44
  catharsis, 10
Freudenberger, Herbert J., 29

G
general adaptation syndrome (GAS), 2
giving up, 10

glucose, 5, 15, 28
gross stress reaction (GSR), 44

H

heart attack, 14
holistic approach, 13
homeostasis, 8
    water and, 14
hypertension, 3, 28

I

immediate stress interventions, 12, 16
immune system
    acute stress and, 5
    antioxidants and, 14
    chronic stress and, 9
    communication and, 17
    effects of massage therapy on, 19
    in long-term alcohol use, 15
independent variable, 63
indirect impact, 57
internally motivated, 27
International Critical Incident Stress Foundation (ICISF), 32, 52

K

Kardiner, Abraham, 43
Korsakoff's syndrome, 15

L

large-scale incident, 36
Lazarus, Richard, 2
learned helplessness, 10
long-term stress intervention, 13, 20

M

major incident, 36
Maslach, Christina, 29
massage therapy, 19
McFarlane, Alexander, 34, 70
meditative prayer, 19
meta-analysis, 65
methylated xanthine, 15
    fight-or-flight, 15
minerals, 14
Mitchell, Jeffery, 27, 32
multiple-casualty incident, 36

N

need-to-help others, 27

O

one-on-one, 52
Ornish, Dean, 9, 14, 17
outcome measures, 64, 68, 72

P

Pavlov, Ivan, 21
Pavlovian conditioning, 21
peripheral vascular disease, 14
personality
    as vulnerable to critical incidents, 69
personality stressors, 26
personality trait, 26
posttraumatic stress disorder (PTSD), 33, 41
    current understanding of, 46
    past terms for, 43
precrisis preparations, 52
premorbid, 44
primary victims, 56
process
    as defined in interactional psychology, 54
process debriefing (PD), 54
    goals of, 54
psychotraumatology, 43

R

randomization, 67
referrals, 57
relying on belief systems, 61
rescue personality, 26

S

Scafer, Walter, 21
scientific method, 62
scientific research
    key elements of, 63, 72
secondary victims, 56
self-report measures, 69
Seligaman, Martin, 10
Selye, Hans, 2, 9
sense of dedication, 28
shift-work, 24, 28
Sigel, Bernie, 21
simple sugars, 15
Skinner, B. F., 21
sleep disorders, 28
social support systems, 28
stress, 2
    acute, 3
    affective reactions, 6
    alcohol and, 15
    behavioral reactions, 7
    chronic, 3
    cognitive reactions, 5
    coping, 9
    defined, 2
    diet and, 13
    distress, 2
    eustress, 2
    exercise and, 16
    four stages of, 3
    general adaptation syndrome, 2
    immediate interventions, 16
    Lazarus, Richard, 2
    neustress, 2
    physiological reactions, 5
    Selye, Hans, 2
stress management, 12
    alcohol and, 15
    art therapy, 21
    behavior modification, 20
    caffeine and, 15
    cognitive restructuring, 20
    communication, 17
    diaphragmatic breathing, 18
    diet and, 13
    exercise and, 16
    holistic approach, 13
    immediate interventions, 16
    massage therapy, 19
    meditative prayer, 19
    things to avoid, 15
stress response, 4
    affective reactions, 6
    as healthy and normal, 9
    as outdated, 9
    behavioral reactions, 7
    cognitive reactions, 5
    communication and, 17
    fight-or-flight, 5
    physiological reactions, 5
    relaxation or exhaustion, 8
stressor, 4
stroke, 14
study design, 63

T

tertiary victims, 56
thromboxane, 14

U

unrealistic optimism, 25

V

vitamins, 14

W

water, 14
Watson, John, 21
Wernicke's encephalopathy, 15